50 BRONZE AGE FINDS
From the Portable Antiquities Scheme

Dot Boughton

AMBERLEY

First published 2021

Amberley Publishing
The Hill, Stroud
Gloucestershire, GL5 4EP

www.amberley-books.com

ISBN 978 1 4456 8201 3 (print)
ISBN 978 1 4456 8202 0 (ebook)

British Library Cataloguing in Publication Data.
A catalogue record for this book is available from the British Library.

Typeset in 10pt on 13pt Celeste.
SJmagic DESIGN SERVICES, India.
Printed in the UK.

Contents

Note and Acknowledgements

Using the chosen fifty Bronze Age finds as a starting point, this book tries to include and describe the main Bronze Age artefact types found in England and Wales. However, due to the sheer number and wealth of British Bronze Age material culture it just was not possible to discuss them all in detail. I have therefore tried to incorporate a mixture of examples of the most common Bronze Age artefact types, as well as the rarest, most spectacular objects and oddities that were recorded with the Portable Antiquities' Finds Liaison Officers in the past two decades. I chose this approach because I am hoping that this book will be used by both archaeologists and finders to help them identify Bronze Age objects found in England and Wales and to promote the brilliant resource that is the Portable Antiquities Database.

Special thanks has to go to all those who provided extra images for this volume, especially Ian Richardson (Treasure Registrar), Dr Tim Pestell (Norfolk), Sabine Skae (Dock Museum, Cumbria), Laura Radcliffe (Cornwall) and Abigail Baker (interim FLO North East).

I would like to dedicate this book to all finders of Bronze Age artefacts in England and Wales, and my friends and former colleagues from the Portable Antiquities Scheme (you are doing an amazing job!), especially my dear friends and fellow Bronze Age enthusiasts Peter Reavill (Herefordshire and Shropshire) and Katie Hinds (Hampshire).

Preface

Since 1997, over 12,000 Bronze Age items have been recorded with the British Museum's Portable Antiquities Scheme (PAS), a project to record archaeological finds made by the public to further interest in archaeology and advance knowledge of the past. It is a formidable number, but actually only a small percentage of the total – less than 1 percent in fact. Nonetheless, Dot Boughton (formerly PAS Finds Liaison Officer for Cumbria and

Fig. 1: Small Late Bronze Age hoard from Eastbourne, East Sussex (SUSS-8F5010), containing two socketed axes, a gouge, a chisel and a few bronze fragments, probably for recycling.

Lancashire) has done a fine job picking her top fifty for us to marvel at – the rest can be found on the PAS database (finds.org.uk) for anyone to search, learn about and enjoy.

For most of us, the Bronze Age (beginning some 4,500 years ago) is a time far off in the human past, but the objects shown in this book help bring these people who made them closer to us. Dominated by tools, such as flint arrowheads, axes and spearheads, it is often hard to look beyond hunting culture, carpentry and warfare. However, items highlighted here, such as their gold jewellery suggest sophisticated people, with a craftsmanship beyond the (seemingly) primitive tools they used, and complex religious beliefs.

Most of the Bronze Age items illustrated here have been found by metal detectorists and it must be an exciting experience for the finders that discover them. I was very lucky to be the Finds Liaison Officer for Kent when the Ringlemere Cup (No. 14) was reported to me under the Treasure Act 1996. It was absolutely amazing to be one of the first people to see it and be involved with its progression from detector find to museum exhibit – I couriered it to London, helped organise the permissions for fieldwork, and helped out on the excavations that followed. Ever since it has had a special place in my heart, and whenever I can, I try and pass through the prehistoric galleries at the British Museum to see it on display.

Not all the finds in this book have ended up in museums, highlighting the essential aim of the PAS: to record finds so that by preservation by record knowledge of these items is made available to all, to advance knowledge and unlock the hidden history of Britain's past.

Prof Michael Lewis
Head, Portable Antiquities & Treasure, British Museum

Foreword

As we admire the fifty wonderful finds that fill these pages, we cannot help but speculate as to how and why they ended up in the ground beneath our feet. Whole woodlands have been sacrificed to answering these questions. As Dr Boughton demonstrates so clearly, the most important approach involves the detailed study and consideration of the objects themselves: their qualities, parallels and contexts. Take, for example, the precious fragment

Fig. 2: A hoard of gold ornaments (body or neck rings and arm-rings) from Crowdown, West Berkshire (BERK-683F91).

of gold lunula from Brampton in Cumbria described in this book (find No. 4). Similar finds have been made across Britain, Ireland and the near Continent. In all cases, they are buried alone or with a limited range of other object types, and they are never placed in graves. Patterns of this type provide the best way of understanding the values and motives of prehistoric people.

If you are new to the objects and culture of the Bronze Age in Britain, then you will find much to impress you in the beautiful and skilfully made objects described in this book, e.g. from Crowdown, West Berkshire. This was no 'dark age' but, rather, a time of accomplished craft, creativity and connectivity – across Britain and with the near Continent. If you already have a good knowledge of the period, you will find yourself in the expert hands of an author who understands the context and significance of these fifty tremendous finds. You are entering into a fascinating period, when the objects that were made and deposited were central to how people expressed their identities, beliefs and connections. Although the period spanned almost 1,600 years (or eighty generation), objects kept traditions and cultures alive, creating links and connections between people. From the pages of this book they reach out to you and provide a window on a world that is both familiar and bravely new.

Dr Neil Wilkin
Curator of the European Bronze Age,
British Museum, 6 April 2020

Chapter 1
Introduction: The British Bronze Age

In the past two decades nearly 12,000 Bronze Age objects and over 400 metalwork hoards were recovered by members of the public and subsequently reported to the Finds Liaison Officers (FLOs) of the Portable Antiquities Scheme (PAS). Among these are items of stone, jet, amber and ceramic, but most of all objects made from copper alloy (bronze). Out of nearly 12,000 single Bronze Age finds recorded with the PAS, over 7,000 were made from copper alloy (Fig. 3) and just over 3,000 were made from stone (Fig. 4). Most copper alloy objects are tools or weapons, but there are also a number of personal ornaments, horse harness and cart fittings, vessels and metalworking debris. Chance discoveries of Bronze Age burials and settlements are very rare; most Bronze Age artefacts recorded with the PAS are single finds or metalwork hoards, with the latter having to be reported under the 2002 Amendment to the Treasure Act (1996).

In calendar years, the British Bronze Age lasted from approximately 2350 BC to 800 BC, and the period conventions used by the Portable Antiquities Scheme are:

- Early Bronze Age: 2350–1600 BC
- Middle Bronze Age: 1600–1000 BC
- Late Bronze Age: 1000–800 BC

These dates are only approximate but they are generally backed up by radio-carbon dates. Also, there is a natural overlap between the individual periods; the calendar dates listed above are merely to facilitate database entry.

Generally, there is no set date for the beginning of the British Bronze Age. Some sources give a date as late as 2000 BC, while others set 2400 BC as the demarcation line between the Late Stone Age (Neolithic) and the Early Bronze Age. In recognition of this difficulty in defining the start of the Early Bronze Age, the centuries between 2500 BC and 2000 BC are generally termed the 'Late Neolithic/Early Bronze Age'. Some archaeologists recognise this transition period as a period in its own right, the 'Copper Age' or 'Chalcolithic'. In this transition period, copper was produced and used on a very small scale. It was not yet alloyed with tin or lead to make any of the different copper alloys used throughout the British Bronze Age and later periods.

Fig. 3: Socketed axes are the most common Bronze Age find recorded on the PAS database. This example was found at Oswestry, rural, Shropshire (LVPL-FA9A48).

Fig. 4: Many smaller Bronze Age tools were still made from stone, often flint, like this thumbnail scraper from Wilby, Suffolk (SF-1F57D2).

The British Early Bronze Age is well known for monuments like the later stages of Stonehenge, but also for the production of beautifully crafted gold objects, such as lunulae and so-called basket ear rings or hair ornaments. Many of these gold objects were crafted from Irish gold. Gold bars were hammered into extremely thin sheets or foil and then decorated by engraving or punching. They were sometimes found in burials, mainly in southern Britain in graves of the Wessex culture.

While the Early Bronze Age was known for the earliest copper-alloy tools, weapons and beautifully crafted gold ornaments, as well as large stone monuments during the Middle Bronze Age, the production of a much more varied bronze metalwork assemblage took off. People produced longer stabbing and slashing weapons such as dirks and rapiers, but also made their enigmatic relations, the large, heavy ceremonial dirks such as the example found near East Rudham, Norfolk (No. 20). The Middle Bronze Age also saw a marked increase of different kinds of woodworking tools made from bronze, such as palstave adzes, chisels and smaller socketed axes and hammers. Unlike the succeeding Late Bronze Age, there is also a very broad spectrum of bronze ornaments (summarised as the 'Ornament Horizon' in southern England), commonly found in metalwork hoards with weapons or palstaves, the dominant axe type of the Middle Bronze Age. Among the ornaments of the Middle Bronze Age – and almost unknown in the Late Bronze Age – are quoit-headed pins, spiral finger rings and large decorated bracelets.

The Late Bronze Age is mainly characterised by the deposition of metalwork hoards in almost all parts of Britain, but especially in South Wales, along the Yorkshire coast, East Anglia and Kent. Fewer hoards are known from northern England and Scotland. Unlike earlier Middle Bronze Age hoards, which also included personal ornaments such as arm-rings or pins, metalwork hoards of the Late Bronze Age mainly contained complete or broken up weapons and tools, mainly socketed axes. Furthermore, the contents of almost all Late Bronze Age hoards tend to have a regional 'flavour' in that certain axe types were produced and deposited in certain regions, such as socketed axes of South Welsh type, Yorkshire three-ribbed axes and South-eastern plain and ribbed axes. Occasional finds of Late Bronze Age bronze also include sheet metal cauldrons and flesh hooks or flesh forks, suggesting not only an increase in regional characterisation seen in the different socketed axes, but also in increase in communal gatherings and feasting – a very important aspect of communal life that started in the Late Bronze Age but would carry on through the Iron Age and later periods until today.

Chapter 2
Bronze Age Metalwork Deposition

Bronze Age artefacts, especially items of metalwork, are predominantly found on their own or in metalwork hoards and much less often in graves, especially in the Middle Bronze Age and Late Bronze Age. Furthermore, our findspot information can be very variable because often only very limited details are known. In the past, many objects and hoards were found accidentally by farmers labouring in the fields or by workmen during activities such as digging for turf, ploughing, quarrying or building; more recently, hoards were discovered by metal detectorists with subsequent excavations by archaeologists. For a number of older finds, information about their depositional context is irretrievably lost but for our modern discoveries, especially with objects found by responsible metal detectorists, we know so much more about the deposition of metalwork hoards: we know the exact location and sometimes even the original layout of the metalwork within the hoard or whether or not they were deposited within a pit, a container or just laid out in the ground.

Prehistoric metalwork hoards are an important context in which metal items are being found (Fig. 1). The 2002 Amendment to the Treasure Act defines that more than two items of prehistoric metalwork found together make up a 'hoard' and must be reported to the local coroner under the Treasure Act (1996).

Both precious and base metal objects can be found in Bronze Age hoards, sometimes together. These are objects made from copper alloy (bronze or brass), gold and, in the very latest hoards, iron (Fig. 5). During the Bronze Age, most hoards included, as the name suggests, items made from bronze, but a number of hoards also contained or were solely made up of gold objects. Hoards could also include, more rarely, objects made of bone, jet, shale, amber or other fossilised plant materials.

The question that still remains unanswered within the archaeological community is why hoards were deposited. What was hoarded and why? Was it for hiding? For safekeeping? As an offering to the deities? Was it meant to be hidden to be retrieved or never to be retrieved again? Most archaeologists are in agreement that the majority of hoards were buried for safekeeping of some kind, and the contents of each hoard could give us a clue as to who may have buried it. 'Personal hoards' were generally smaller, with more diverse, 'personalised' contents and possible heirlooms while larger assemblages could be viewed as more impersonal collections, i.e. the stock-in-trade of a merchant or possibly a metalworker's toolkit. A third category, 'merchants' hoards', was supposed to include mainly unworked, unbroken artefacts.

Even though the reason for any deposition may be disputed by some, archaeologists generally agree that it is extremely significant where objects were hidden or deposited. It may be of special significance if hoards were hidden or deposited in retrievable or irretrievable places. Bronze Age hoards could have been deposited in what archaeologists call wet (i.e. rivers, lakes, bogs, swamps, etc) or dry places. Interpretation of artefacts deposited on dry land can be difficult as there is usually a more complicated structure to the deposition such as the distinction between settlement, hoards or single finds. This last group of artefacts found in isolation may have come from a multitude of different locations, for example near or hilltops, near mountain passes, near lakes, rivers or rock fissures. While depositions in close proximity to known lowland settlements are rare, hill forts and monuments played a more significant role. Furthermore, hoards may have been deposited in wet places subsequently drained, thus making the irretrievable retrievable (Fig. 6).

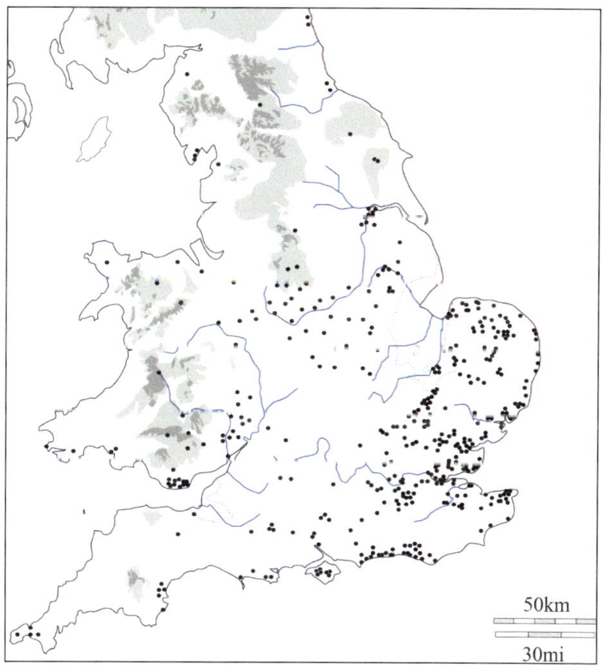

Above left: Fig. 5: A Late Bronze Age hoard containing gold and bronze items: the Rossett Hoard, now at Wrexham Museum (Treasure Number 2002T300).

Above right: Fig. 6: Distribution of Late Bronze Age metalwork hoards reported as treasure and recorded with the Portable Antiquities Scheme (Map: D. Boughton 2020).

Chapter 3
The Copper Age/ Chalcolithic Period

The British Chalcolithic period, or Copper Age, dates from *c.* 2500 BC to 2150 BC. The term is used by some to describe the very short transitional period between the Late Neolithic and the Early Bronze Age. As a prehistoric period in its own right, it has been much debated among researchers. However, it cannot be denied that important changes happened during that period and these are reflected in its material culture. In the Chalcolithic, the first simple metal items appear in Britain: objects made from copper and gold, often copying Late Neolithic predecessors that were made from stone (Fig. 7). There was also a new ceramic tradition, called 'Beakers' after their characteristic pots. During this transition period we can observe a marked change in burial tradition and personal ornamentation that can be found in many (but not all) regions of the British Isles at that time. The Chalcolithic marks a time of social and cultural change and the movement of people and ideas into this country.

Fig. 7: Chalcolithic/Copper Age flint dagger from Horwich, Bolton (LVPL-F7E419). Length: 141 mm.

1. Dagger (LANCUM-3BEC10)
Chalcolithic (*c.* 2450–2150 BC)
Length: 110.5 mm Width: 29 mm Thickness: 0.95 mm Weight: 20.78 g
Silverdale, Lancashire

Chalcolithic tanged daggers can be difficult to identify. They are often plain and lack a midrib or other defining features like our dagger from Silverdale, Lancashire (LANCUM-3BEC10 (Fig. 8). Other examples were recorded from Witton Gilbert, County Durham (NCL-093B77), East Dorset (DOR-FCCD7E) and Newport, West Midlands (HESH-7C7854).

Although bronze use became widespread for blades such as dagger and knives during the Chalcolithic and Early Bronze Age, highly skilled flint knappers still produced flint daggers such as these beautiful examples from Uplands near Swansea (NMGW-F4A584, Fig. 9) and Heptonstall (Calderdale, SWYOR-AABE73) dating from *c.* 2400 to 2200 BC. The position of the notching implies a hafting technique based on organic plates either side of the tang.

The hilts of the early bronze blades were also made from an organic material such as antler, bone or wood. In later daggers, the hilt plates were often held in place by small bronze rivets like this example from Upham, Hampshire (HAMP-D83C03, Fig. 10). Sadly, organic hilts very rarely survive. Sometimes, the outline of the hilt is preserved in the metal surface of the dagger, and also there are rivet holes showing us where the hilt was attached to the blade. Two slightly later daggers that still retain the hilt outline were recorded from Dent, Cumbria (LANCUM 93130B), and the Isle of Wight (IOW-BD52F2). They both date from the Early Bronze Age (c. 1700–1500 BC) and are of Camerton-Snowshill type.

Above left: Fig. 8: A Chalcolithic/Copper Age bronze dagger from Silverdale, Lancashire (LANCUM 3BEC10).

Above right: Fig. 9: Flint dagger from Uplands, near Swansea (NMGW-F4A584).

Right: Fig. 10: Bronze rivet from Upham, Hampshire (HAMP-D83C03).

2. Copper flat axe (PUBLIC-569DE1)
Chalcolithic (*c.* 2300–2050 BC)
Length: 109.2 mm Weight: 356.1 g Width (blade): 67 mm Thickness: 2 mm
Tintern, Monmouthshire

The earliest flat axes, of the British Brithdir and Willerby metalwork traditions and dating from the very Early Bronze Age, were made from nearly 100 per cent copper. One example, found near Tintern in Monmouthshire and recorded as PUBLIC-569DE1 was analysed metallurgically and the result showed the axe to be predominantly copper at 99.2–99.8 per cent (Fig. 11). Trace elements of arsenic, tin and antimony were also detected, with averages of 0.23 per cent, 0.14 per cent and 0.23 percent respectively. The flat axe from Tintern is complete. The butt is thin or sharp and arched. Both faces are convex, giving the axe a lenticular body profile. There is no median bevel or blade facet on the faces, although the blade narrows sharply to the edge. The faces are flat across their widths, gradually becoming increasing convex towards the blade edge. The sides of the axe are straight and divergent along the upper half of the axe and are concave along the blade, turning out sharply at the ends to produce blade tips. The blade edge is strongly curved. The surface of the axe has a mid-green surface with areas of dark-brown surface loss.

A slenderer parallel for this copper flat axe comes from Dent, Cumbria, recorded as LANCUM-E3C336 (Fig. 12).

Fig. 11: Copper flat axe from Tintern, Monmouthshire (PUBLIC-569DE1).

Fig. 12: Copper flat axe from Dent, Cumbria (LANCUM E3C336).

3. Gold basket earrings or hair tresses (BERK-F548E6)
Chalcolithic (*c.* 2500–220 0BC)
Ornament 1: Length: 35.90 mm 4.66 mm Weight: 1.1 g.
Ornament 2: Length: 32.00 mm Length of tab: 3.26 mm Weight: 1.1 g.
Whitchurch, Hampshire

A class of objects that belongs to the earliest phases of metallurgy in Britain is that of the so-called 'basket ornaments'. These enigmatic objects are usually associated with burials and date from the earliest phase of the Bronze Age, *c.* 2400–2200 BC. They are variously referred to as 'basket ornaments', 'basket earrings', 'hair rings' or 'hair tresses'. They are in any case personal ornaments, and have been found in pairs in graves dating to the early Beaker period. Whether worn on hair, ears or items of costume, they were rolled into a basket shape in use. They were cut from very thin gold sheet and shaped into an elongated oval shape with long tang or projection sticking out at a right angle from one of the long sides. They are often decorated on one side only with small punched dots or incised lines (e.g. GLO-92912E, Fig. 14). Although the two from Whitchurch were found as a pair (Fig. 13), there are several examples of singular discoveries of basket ornaments that have been tightly folded, such as the example from Kirkhaugh in Northumberland (DUR-02828D, Fig. 14). One example from Chalbourn on the Isle of White is missing its tang but the foil has been pierced twice near the break (IOW-B16625, Fig. 15). The non-destructive X-ray

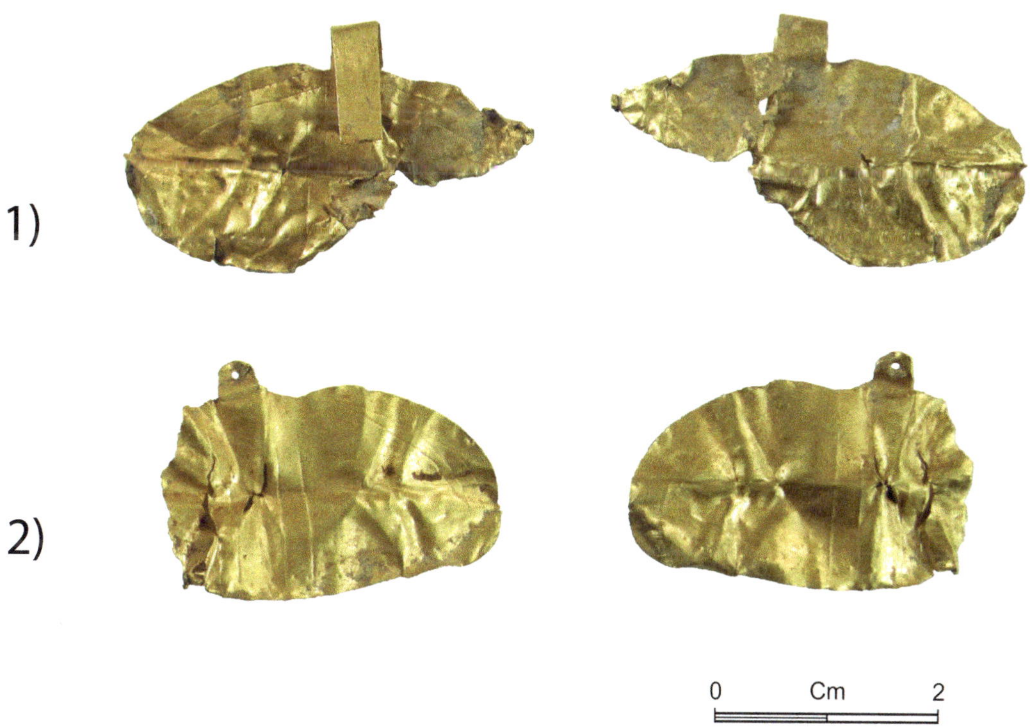

Fig. 13: Two gold 'basket earrings' or 'hair tresses' from Whitchurch, Hampshire (BERK-F548E6).

fluorescence analysis of the surface of a basket ornament from Cholsey, Oxfordshire (BERK-oD1A05), indicated a gold content of approximately 90–92 per cent, a silver content of approximately 7–8 per cent, with less than 1 per cent copper detectable at the surface (Fig. 14, left below). A similar yet different contemporary object – a gold button – was found near Cobham in Kent (KENT-5C3F42, Fig. 15). It too was made from sheet gold, with a double perforation placed slightly off-centre and a decoration consisting of five roughly executed concentric grooves surrounding a central zone containing lightly punched dots.

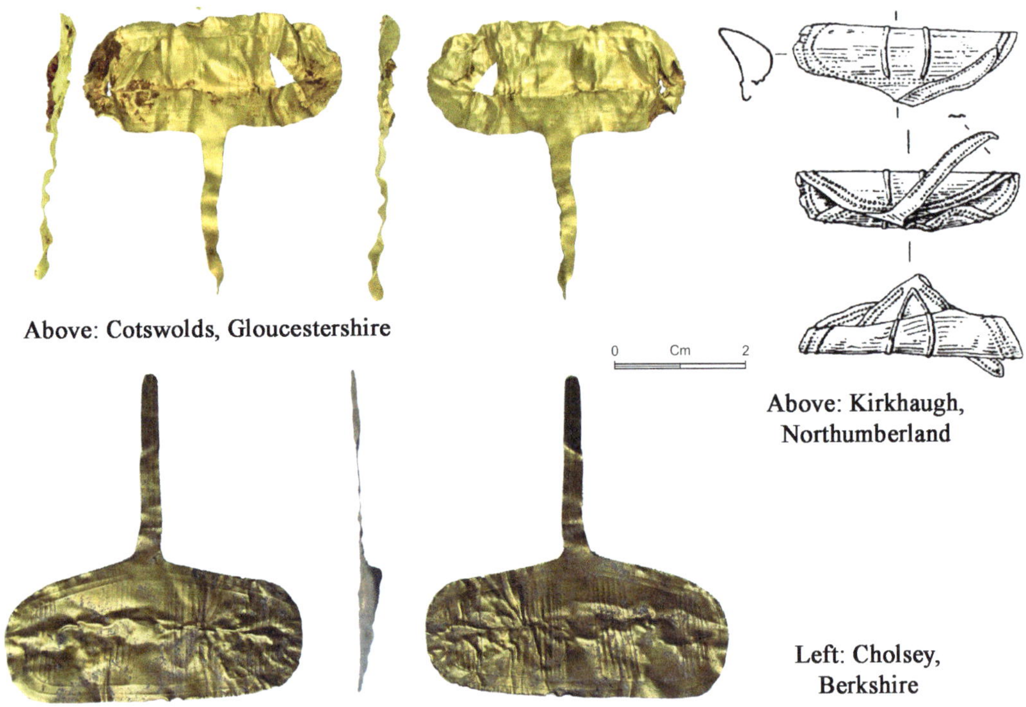

Above: Fig. 14: Three examples of gold 'basket earrings' or 'hair tresses' from the Cotswolds, Gloucestershire (above left: GLO-92912E); Cholsey, Berkshire (below left: BERK-oD1A05) and Kirkhaugh, Northumberland (above right: DUR-02828D).

Left: Fig. 15: Gold 'basket earring' or 'hair tress' from Calbourne, Isle of Wight (left: IOW-B16625) and gold 'button' from Cobham, Kent (right: KENT-5C3F42).

4. Lunula fragment (LANCUM-449151)
Chalcolithic (*c.* 2400–2000 BC)
Length: 47.48 mm Width: 25.97 mm Width: 0.63 mm Weight: 6.86 g
Brampton, Cumbria

Although common in Ireland, lunulae are very rare Bronze Age gold objects found in the British Isles and north-west France. They date from around 2400–2000 BC and were large, very thin crescent- (hence 'lunula') shaped neck ornaments. The terminals, possibly used to interlock and secure the crescent-shaped collar behind the wearer's neck, were the strongest and heaviest elements of the lunula and probably prone to breaking or snapping off. This is what may have happened to a lunula terminal found near Brampton in Cumbria (LANCUM-449151, Fig. 16). This terminal (or 'horn') consists of a flat part, which is shaped like the bowl of a spoon, which is connected by a short 'stalk' to an elongated part with flat-rectangular cross-section, which would have extended into the large, crescent-shaped collar. The bowl-shaped end is undecorated on both sides, but the strip displays a decoration of parallel lines on the obverse while being undecorated on the reverse.

Fig. 16: Gold lunula terminal from Brampton, Cumbria (LANCUM-449151).

This is the first lunula fragment from Cumbria. Only few are known from Scotland and a small number were found in Cornwall and Brittany, France. In contrast to some of the Scottish lunulae and this new fragment from Brampton, original Irish lunulae were made from extremely thin gold sheet (less than 0.1 mm thick). They are very fragile and much less substantial than these thicker lunulae known as 'Provincial lunulae'. As far as we can tell from old find reports and museum records, most lunulae were found singly or, rarer, in pairs, deposited on their own or possibly in a box or pouch. Usually complete, lunulae have not been found within clear grave or hoard contexts and are thus generally considered to be single depositions.

Only two (almost) complete lunulae have been reported to the PAS so far: one from near Thwing in the East Riding of Yorkshire (DUR-A24C08, Fig. 17) and the other from the Tarrant Valley in Dorset (DOR-2198F8, Fig. 18). The latter findspot is unusual because most of the previous discoveries were made in coastal or upland locations.

Fig. 17: Folded and crumpled gold lunula from Thwing, East Riding of Yorkshire (DUR-A24C08).

Fig. 18: A near complete gold lunula from Tarrant Valley, Dorset (DOR-2198F8).

5. Jet bead (KENT-A5B841)
Chalcolithic/Early Bronze Age (*c.* 2000–1800 BC)
Length: 44.7 mm Width: 26.2 mm Thickness: 6.6mm Weight: 5.6 g
Boughton Monchelsea, Kent

Natural occurring jet, a form of lignite, was used in the Early Bronze Age to make single beads as well as flat spacer beads. Jet is formed when wood decomposed under high pressure millions of years ago. The material is soft and can be carved and its surface polished resulting in a very shiny black object. Jet was used to create this large flat terminal spacer bead found near Boughton Monchelsea, Kent (KENT-A5B841, Fig. 19). It was made for a jet spacer plate necklace, which originally may have had up to six larger spacer beads and possibly over a hundred smaller jet beads in between the spacer beads. The terminal spacer bead is trapezoidal in shape and sub-rectangular in cross section. There is a circular drilled perforation at the pointed terminal through which single thread would be attached. There are three further circular perforations on the reverse surface, which travel through the bead at approximately 45 degrees and emerge on the bottom edge. A separate thread would be attached to each hole allowing three strings of beads to emerge from the spacer bead. The upper surface is decorated with lines of punched circular depressions forming a triangular design; the design seems to be indicating where the strings meet the attachment hole. There is damage around three of the attachment holes, which could be a sign of wear. Due to the crescent-shaped arrangement of jet beads in this type of ornament, it is generally thought that they copy (in shape and design) contemporary gold lunulae (see No.4, Fig. 18).

Early Bronze Age jet beads are rare finds and only four have been recorded with the PAS, one of which is this large fragment from Ravenstonedale, Cumbria (LANCUM-AF6483, Fig. 20).

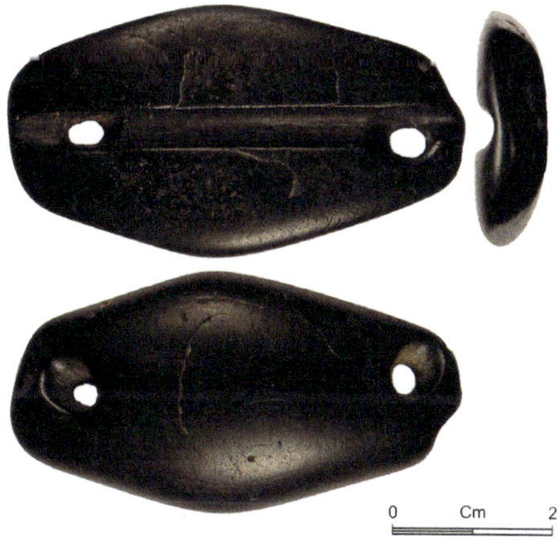

Above left: Fig. 19: Terminal jet spacer bead from Boughton Monchelsea, Kent (KENT-A5B841).

Above right: Fig. 20: Reworked jet bead from Ravenstonedale, Cumbria (LANCUM-AF6483).

6. Barbed-and-tanged arrowhead (IOW-FB307D)
Chalcolithic/Early Bronze Age (*c.* 2500–1500 BC)
Length: 32.5 mm Width: 24.9 mm Thickness: 5 mm Weight: 3.21 g
Cowes, Isle of Wight

Barbed-and-tanged arrowheads are common finds from the British Chalcolithic and Early Bronze Age. They are securely dated because sixteen of them were found in the grave of Wiltshire's Amesbury Archer, alongside vessels of the characteristic Beaker pottery, stone bracers (see No. 7) and gold hair ornaments (see No. 4). The majority of barbed-and-tanged arrowheads was skilfully knapped from flint, but there are also rare examples made from chert or volcanic tuff – the same material Neolithic Langdale axes were made from. They were found in all regions and often locally sourced flint of different colours were used, for example Cowes, Isle of Wight (IOW-FB307D, Fig. 21); Elvaston, Derbyshire (DENO-76ED57, Fig. 22); Ripponden, Yorkshire (SWYOR-DoB745, Fig. 23C); Rimpton, Somerset (SOM-4E4545, Fig. 23B); and Charlwood, Surrey (SUR-8DE6E2, Fig. 23A). These flint arrowheads look identical to barbed and tanged arrowheads made from bronze, but bronze arrowheads are much rarer and date from a later period than their Chalcolithic lookalikes (see No. 14).

Above left: Fig. 21: Flint barbed-and-tanged arrowhead from Cowes, Isle of Wight (IOW-FB307D).

Above right: Fig. 22: Flint barbed-and-tanged arrowhead from Elvaston, Derbyshire (DENO-76ED57).

Left: Fig. 23: Three flint barbed-and-tanged arrowheads. A: Charlwood, Surrey (SUR-8DE6E2). B: Rimpton, Somerset (SOM-4E4545). C: Ripponden, Yorkshire (SWYOR-DoB745).

7. Bracer/wrist guard (CORN-B40E87)
Late Neolithic/Chalcolithic (*c.* 2500–2000 BC)
Length: 81 mm Width: 27 mm Thickness: 8 mm Weight: 30.5 g
Walsingham, Norfolk

The famous grave of the Amesbury Archer (Wiltshire) also included a flat stone artefact that had been placed by his lower left arm (or he was wearing it at the time of burial). This artefact has been identified as a bracer or wrist guard, which would protect the skin on the inside of the archer's arm from the recoil of the bow's string after shooting the arrow. Bracers were made from stone and bracer fragments are often difficult to identify unless they have the characteristic drilled holes along the narrow sides, such as these examples from Walsingham, Norfolk (CORN-B40E87, Fig. 24), and Paul, Cornwall (CORN-B38773, Fig. 25).

The bracer from Walsingham was made from grey-green, very fine grained metamorphic rock (amphibolite), which is harder than a steel point. Stone bracers such as these often have between one and three perforations along the narrower sides, presumably for attachment to the lower arm. However, there is a number of 'bracers' from burials where they have been placed or worn on the outside of the arm or in the region of the upper arm, suggesting that when worn they had no practical but potentially a symbolic use. The current view is that many of them would have been valuable items that were mounted on the outer arm where they acted as highly visible signs of status.

Above: Fig. 24: Stone wrist guard from Walsingham, Norfolk (CORN-B40E87).

Right: Fig. 25: Stone wrist guard from Paul, Cornwall (CORN-B38773).

8. Thumbnail scraper (SOM-6BB778)
Chalcolithic/Early Bronze Age (*c.* 2500–1500 BC)
Length: 32.4 mm Width: 29.2 mm Thickness: 9.3 mm Weight: 9.9 g
Over Compton, Dorset

During the Early Bronze Age people still used – and often favoured – small flint tools. Barbed-and-tanged arrowheads are a good example and very skilled flint knappers produced beautiful flint daggers (see Nos 1 and 6).

The most common flint tools in use at that time are scrapers, such as this example called a 'thumbnail' scraper (for its size and shape) from Over Compton, Dorset (SOM-6BB778, Fig. 26), which was made from a tertiary flint flake. At the upper end on the reverse is a bulb of percussion and a marked bulbar scar. Ripples radiate down the reverse. On the obverse there are a number of flaking scars and the lower end has been abruptly retouched. Thumbnail scrapers such as the example from Over Compton and another find from Arreton, Isle of Wight (IOW-2FCA7A, Fig. 27B) were knapped from small flint cores. Another example comes from Deal (Kent), recorded as KENT-47848E (Fig 27A). The core is irregularly shaped with two striking platforms at right angles. The core has distinctive 'tortoise shell' flaking typical of a much earlier, Middle-Palaeolithic (Old Stone Age) Levalloisian production technique, but this later core is much smaller than cores and tools being produced during the Middle-Palaeolithic, which strongly suggests that this old knapping technique was still known and being used during the Early Bronze Age.

Other beautifully knapped and retouched flint tools that span the Later Neolithic and Early Bronze Age are plano-convex knives such as the examples recorded from Laneshaw Bridge, Lancashire (LANCUM-DA9AF5, Fig. 28A), and Nuneaton, Warwickshire (WMID-7EDC53, Fig. 28B).

Fig. 26: 'Thumbnail' scraper from Over Compton, Dorset (SOM-6BB778).

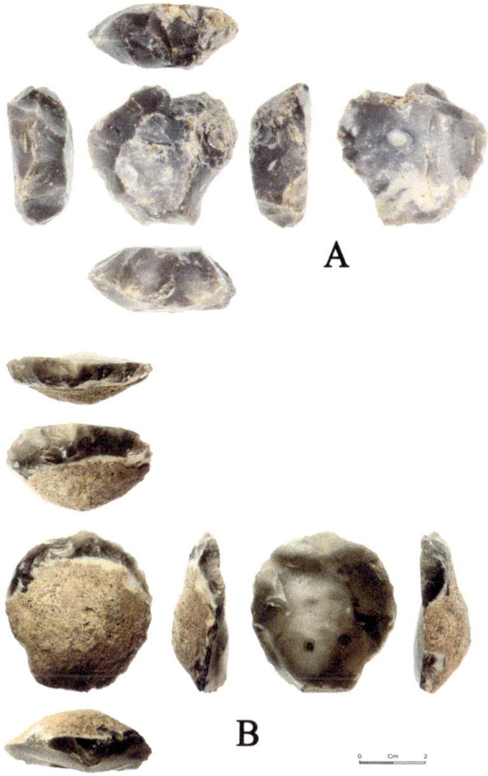

Fig. 27: Thumbnail scrapers from (A) Deal, Kent (KENT-47848E) and (B) Arreton, Isle of Wight (IOW-2FCA7A).

Fig. 28: (A) Laneshaw Bridge, Lancashire (LANCUM-DA9AF5) and (B) Nuneaton, Warwickshire (WMID-7EDC53).

Chapter 4
The Early Bronze Age (*c.* 2350–1600 BC)

The people of the British Copper and Early Bronze Age produced a number of very beautifully crafted objects, especially in gold, such as lunulae and objects identified as basket earrings or hair ornaments. This earliest phase of gold working in Britain is characterised by sheet-working techniques together with the use of incised geometric patterns and punched or embossed decoration. The ornaments produced with this metalworking technique are mainly lunulae and discs, but other objects, such as armlets, basket-shaped ornaments, plaques, pendant and beads were also created. Gold items were sometimes found in burials, mainly in southern Britain in graves of the Wessex culture.

Early Bronze Age people often buried their dead under barrows, first using inhumation and later cremation, sometimes in vessels called 'collared urns'. Often these burials were furnished with rich grave goods. The inhabitants of Britain also appear to have had wide ranging trade network, linking them with Continental Europe. They imported amber from the Baltic, jewellery from modern-day Germany, gold from Brittany and daggers and beads from Mycenaean Greece. The wealth from such trade probably permitted the people of southern England, commonly known as people of the Wessex culture, to construct the later phases of Stonehenge, which also indicates a powerful form of social organisation.

9. Perforated object (LANCUM-35CCF6)
Early Bronze Age (*c.* 2500–1500 BC)
Length: 225 mm Width: 115.1 mm Thickness: 56.5 mm
Greysouthen, Cumbria

A number of so-called 'perforated objects' have been recorded with the PAS – such as this example from Greysouthen, Cumbria (LANCUM-35CCF6, Fig. 29). A similar one was recorded from Sleighford, Staffordshire (WMID-030088, Fig. 30B), but there are others, with one side shaped like a 'hammer-head', such as the example from Hopton Wafers, Shropshire (HESH-191F76, Fig. 30A). The term 'perforated object' is often chosen for want of a better word to describe this diverse group of objects, which includes objects such as perforated adzes, axes, hammers and clubs. They may be round, oval or rounded rectangular in shape, with blunt or sharp sides or a 'hammer head', but the one feature they all share is that they have a shaft hole through the vertical axis, presumably for attaching the 'head' to a haft or shaft. However, occasionally the perforation has a surprisingly small diameter, such as on the object from Codford, Wiltshire (WILT-3AC67D, Fig. 31), and appears too small to hold a shaft that would be strong enough to wield the heavy head. In the past these objects were often identified as 'battle axes', 'ceremonial axes' or 'ceremonial clubs', but the classifications are extremely uncertain and the artefact type as a whole is in need of reassessment in line with modern discoveries and approaches to artefact studies. However, they are sufficiently similar in shape and size to be grouped together. Furthermore, they resemble finely worked axes found in Early Bronze Age burials (see No. 10) and are therefore generally thought to be related to those in use and date.

Fig. 29: Perforated object from Greysouthen, Cumbria (LANCUM-35CCF6).

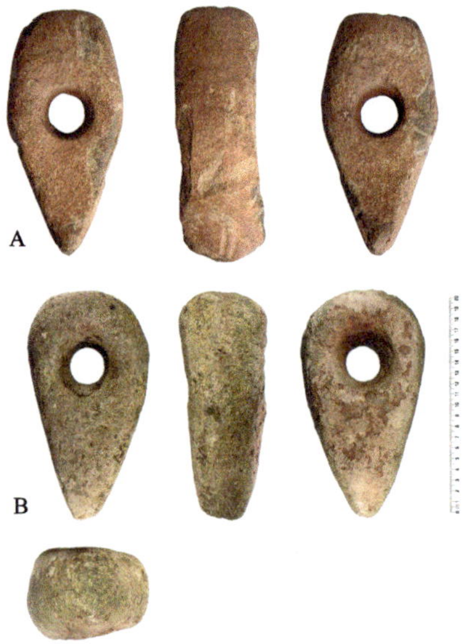

Left: Fig. 30: Perforated objects or 'axe hammers' from (A) Hopton Wafers, Shropshire (HESH-191F76) and (B) Sleighford, Staffordshire (WMID-030088).

Below: Fig. 31: Perforated object from Codford, Wiltshire (WILT-3AC67D).

10. Burial Urns (SWYOR-C4F166; Treasure Number: 2007T388)
Early Bronze Age (*c.* 2020–1750 BC)
Four vessels (three urns, one accessory vessel)
Stanbury, Bradford; acquired by Cliffe Castle Museum, Keighley.

In 2007, during garden alterations at Stanbury near Bradford, landscapers discovered a discrete pit that contained an Early Bronze Age funerary deposit. As soon as the top of the largest urn was uncovered, the work was stopped and archaeologists were called in to excavate the context. This deposit consisted of three large funerary urns: two were nearly complete and a third one was broken. The largest urn had been deposited upside down and the base was damaged during machine excavation. However, from its interior, a stone 'battle-axe' and cremated human bone were recovered. The two near-complete urns were block-lifted (wrapped in plaster bandages) (Figs 32 and 33), while the broken urn was excavated in situ. The block-lifted urns were X-rayed prior to micro-excavation and consolidation by a conservator. During micro-excavation, the largest urn revealed significant quantities of cremated human bone, a bone 'belt-hook', a bone pin, two copper-alloy objects and an ancillary or accessory vessel (Fig. 32). West Yorkshire Archaeology Advisory Service provided the necessary funds to allow the pit to be excavated and the artefacts lifted, conserved and analysed, while English Heritage organised the radiocarbon dating of the human bone. Radiocarbon dating confirms deposition in the date range 2020 to 1770 BC.

Above left: Fig. 32: Burial urns from Stanbury, near Bradford (SWYOR-C4F166).

Above right: Fig. 33: Burial Urns from Stanbury, near Bradford (SWYOR-C4F166).

Fig. 34: Twisted string or cord impressions on a sherd from Winchester, Hampshire (HAMP-9427DC).

Early Bronze Age vessels such as these are called 'collared urns' after their tall upper section resembling an overturned collar, which offers a large surface area for decoration. Consequently, the collar and upper sections of these vessels are often decorated with geometrical designs: zigzags, crisscross, chevron and lines or patterns made using twisted string or cord impressions (such as on this sherd from Winchester, Hampshire (HAMP-9427DC, Fig. 34). Broken pieces of collared urns are often chunky and may have been grog-tempered; breaks also often show large pebble or grit inclusions.

11. Flat axe (PUBLIC-569DE1)
Early Bronze Age (*c.* 2300–2050 BC)
Length: 109.02 mm Width: 67 mm Thickness: 12.5 mm Weight: 356.1 g
Tintern, Monmouthshire

Copper and copper-alloy axes are undoubtedly the most iconic Bronze Age objects. They occur from the Early Bronze Age to the earliest Iron Age and generally follow an evolutionary pattern from flat axes over flanged axes to palstaves and socketed axes. The earliest metal axes were flat axes made from almost 100 per cent copper, like this example from Tintern, Monmouthshire (PUBLIC-569DE1, Fig. 35), which contained 99.2–99.8 per cent copper, with traces of arsenic (0.23 per cent), tin (0.14per cent) and antimony (0.23 per cent). Typologically it is of Ballybeg/Roseisle type, which date to *c.* 2300–2050 BC. The early axes strongly resemble their stone predecessors with convex bodies, lenticular-shaped cross sections and not very widely splayed blades – see also another example from Laughton, Lincolnshire (YORYM-C26951, Fig. 36). The later flat axes start to develop side flanges (giving the axe a H-shaped cross-section) and a stop ridge across the centre, which help to secure the haft, for example on the axes from Sambourne, Warwickshire (WAW-2779F8, Fig. 37A) and Fradley and Streethley in Staffordshire (WMID-2260B2, Fig. 37B). Later developed flat axes are sometimes decorated with dots, zigzags or simple 'rain' patterns, such as on this example from Shap, Cumbria (LANCUM-61F4B3).

Above left: Fig. 35: A flat axe from Tintern, Monmouthshire (PUBLIC-569DE1).

Above right: Fig. 36: Flat axe from Laughton, Lincolnshire (YORYM-C26951).

Right: Fig. 37: Flat axes from (A) Sambourne, Warwickshire (WAW-2779F8) and (B) Fradley and Streethley, Staffordshire (WMID-2260B2).

12. Flanged axe
Early Bronze Age (*c.* 1725–1500 BC)
Length: 122 mm Width: 60.5 mm Thickness: 12.5 mm Weight: 250.3 g
Cowbridge, Glamorgan

At the very end of the Early Bronze Age flanges are added to the sides of axes, presumably to improve how the haft or handle was secured. The flanges could run along almost the entire length of side of the axe or just over half its length – hence the use of the descriptive terms 'long-flanged' and 'short-flanged' axes. Flanged axes in general therefore have a H-shaped cross section, as can see seen on the examples from Cowbridge, Vale of Glamorgan (NMGW-C21D78, Fig. 38), and Amesbury, Wiltshire (WILT-178257: Fig. 39). The height of the flanges and overall form of the axe from Cowbridge means that it can be classed as a long-flanged axe, which is part of the Early Bronze Age Arreton metalwork assemblage (*c.* 1725–1500 BC). The bevel on the axe is quite unusual and can be considered a 'stop-bump', which anticipates the technological development of full stop ridges as seen on later flanged axes (specifically palstaves No. 15). On the very latest flanged axes, stop ridges are added, as on the example from Nether Alderley, Cheshire East (LVPL-C7CF65, Fig. 40A). Flanged axes are more rarely decorated than flat axes, but occasionally, the outside of the flanges are decorated with a moulded pattern (Heptonstall, Yorkshire, SWYOR-3923D4, Fig. 40B).

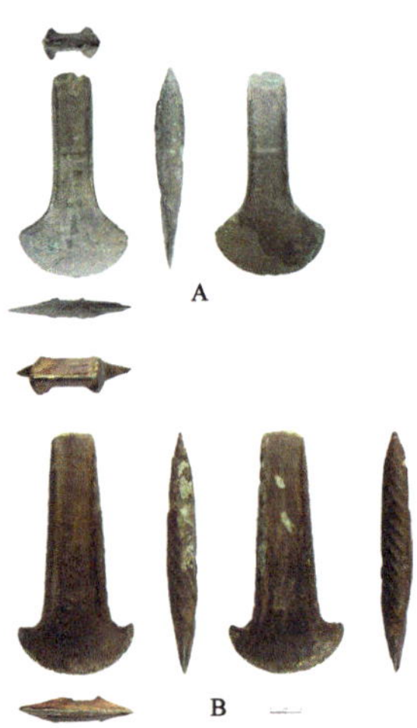

Above left: Fig. 38: Flanged axe from Cowbridge, Vale of Glamorgan (NMGW-C21D78).

Above right: Fig. 39: Flanged axe from Amesbury, Wiltshire (WILT-178257).

Left: Fig. 40: Flanged axes from (A) Nether Alderley, Cheshire East (LVPL-C7CF65) and (B) Heptonstall, Yorkshire (SWYOR-3923D4).

13. Tanged spearhead (IOW-221956)
Early Bronze Age (*c.* 1650–1500 BC)
Length: 98 mm Width: 17.5 mm Thickness: 5 mm Weight: 10.84 g
Shalfleet, Isle of Wight

Tanged spearheads of the Early Bronze Age are much rarer than their socketed Middle and Late Bronze Age successors. The small example from Shalfleet, Isle of Wight (IOW-221956, Fig. 41), is, like the others, part of the Early Bronze Age Arreton metalwork assemblage and dates from *c.* 1650–1500 BC. The spearhead is symmetrical and has a leaf-shaped blade. From its pointed tip the blade flares evenly outwards and downwards towards a rounded base. On both faces of the blade, a longitudinal mid-rib extends from the tip to the base. At the base, the tang extends downwards; it has a roughly rectangular cross-section. At the attachment end of the tang, on the front and rear faces, there is a shallow central longitudinal groove, which may have been created as a result of an imperfection in the mould. The piece is in fair condition and has small areas of superficial corrosion, although the majority of the surfaces have a mid to dark green patina. A much more fragmentary example (where only the tang survives) was found near Pickering, Yorkshire (DUR-2372A1, Fig. 42). This tanged spearhead has a slightly different shape in that the blade base has a protruding ridge or rib that is not present on other tanged spearheads. This, however, is found on some of the early socketed spearheads. A very nice example – complete with rivet – was recovered from Cowbridge, Vale of Glamorgan (NMGW-0BF252, Fig.43). The spearhead is near complete with a distorted tang and leaf-shaped blade. A separate, circular-sectioned rivet with slightly expanded ends remains in place at the bottom end of the tang. Little of the original blade edge survives but they appear to have been straight and gradually converging to the tip. No applied decoration or any evidence for use is present.

Above left: Fig. 41: Tanged spearhead from Shalfleet, Isle of Wight (IOW-221956).

Above middle: Fig. 42: Tanged spearhead fragment from Pickering, Yorkshire (DUR-2372A1).

Above right: Fig. 43: Tanged spearhead from Cowbridge, Glamorgan (NMGW-0BF252).

14. Gold cup (PAS-BE40C2)
Early Bronze Age (*c.* 1950–1750 BC)
Length: 112 mm Width: 105 mm Thickness: 1 mm Weight: 183.7 g
Ringlemere, Kent

This beautiful gold cup from Ringlemere, Kent (PAS-BE40C2: Fig. 44), is one of a small group of six stylistically related gold cups and only the second example of its type to come from Britain. The other British example was found at Rillaton, Cornwall (Fig. 45), while the Continental finds come from Brittany, north-west Germany and northern Switzerland. Generally, the cups have a conical body tapering to an omphalos base; the rim is flaring. The cup found at Ringlemere has a riveted strap handle with lozenge-shaped rivets and decorative ridges on the handle. The rim bears a row of dots punched from the outer surface and is otherwise plain. However, between the plain zone and a further plain zone at the base of the cup is corrugated. Unlike other examples, it was not found undamaged: the vessel was badly crushed when discovery, particularly on one side. However, this damage was very likely recent and may have been caused by a single blow from agricultural machinery.

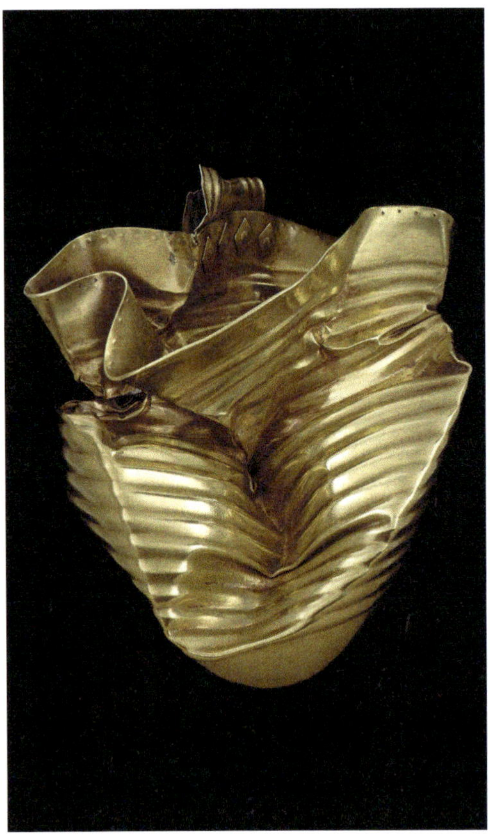

Left: Fig. 44: The Ringlemere Cup (Kent, PAS-BE40C2).

Above: Fig. 45: The Rillaton Cup (Cornwall) After Evans 1881.

Chapter 5
The Middle Bronze Age (*c.* 1600–1000 BC)

The Middle Bronze Age in Britain saw a great increase in the range of bronze metalwork being produced. Cornwall was a major source of tin for Britain and much of western Europe and copper was extracted from sites such as the Great Orme mine in northern Wales. Social groups appear to have been tribal but with growing complexity and hierarchies becoming apparent. The most common tool was undoubtedly the palstave axe, which was a development from the flat and flanged axes of the Early Bronze Age, and while smaller daggers and knives were still used, in combat they were replaced by dirks and rapiers. Generally speaking, weapons and the toolkit diversified and even though some projectiles, such as barbed-and-tanged arrowheads, were still predominantly made from stone, many other weapons and tools, like axes, adzes, chisels, knives and awls, were now being produced in bronze.

People still carried out specialised gold work, which in this period is characterised by sheet-working and bar-working techniques. Ornaments produced with the sheet-working technique were decorated with repoussé or incised decoration, such as armlets and bracelets, while the objects obtained by bar-working techniques were decorated by twisting the body, resulting in ornaments such as body rings, torcs and bracelets.

During the second half of the Middle Bronze Age, the so-called Deverel-Rimbury culture began to emerge (*c.* 1400–1100 BC).

Fig. 46: The Middle Bronze Age hoard from Usk, Monmouthshire (NMGW-39F32DO).

15. Bronze barbed-and-tanged arrowhead (WMID-CE6A76)
Middle Bronze Age (*c.* 1275–1140 BC)
Length: 42 mm Width: 28 mm Thickness: 12.5 mm Weight: 250.3 g
Easenhall, Warwickshire

Only around thirty examples of bronze barbed-and-tanged arrowheads have been recorded from England and Wales. They bear a striking resemblance to Early Bronze Age barbed-and-tanged flint arrowheads (see No. 6), but date from the Middle Bronze Age rather than the Early Bronze Age. There are examples from Salisbury, Wiltshire (WILT-807272, Fig. 48), and Easenhall, Warwickshire (WMID-CE6A76, Fig. 47), on the database, the latter of which only survives incomplete with the tip missing. The arrowhead from Salisbury, however, is complete, although the tip is blunt. Most of these bronze barbed-and-tanged arrowheads are comparatively thin, like an example from Frampton, Dorset (WILT-8171F0, Fig. 49). They also often lack a distinct midrib and rarely have a bevelled edge such as on the example from Easenhall. Their dating is not straightforward with only one bronze arrowhead recorded from a secure context: it was part of the Penard Hoard (West Glamorgan, Wales), which dates from the Middle Bronze Age. At the time of the hoard's discovery the arrowhead was a unique find in Britain and was presumed to be an import as there are numerous finds of bronze arrowheads recorded from northern France. However, the growing number of bronze arrowheads from England and Wales are now casting doubt on this: it is much more likely that they were produced on both sides of the Channel.

Above left: Fig. 47: Bronze barbed-and-tanged arrowhead from Easenhall, Warwickshire (WMID-CE6A76).

Above right: Fig. 48: Bronze barbed-and-tanged arrowhead from Salisbury, Wiltshire (WILT-807272).

Left: Fig. 49: Bronze barbed-and-tanged arrowhead from Frampton, Dorset (WILT-8171F0).

16. Palstave (WMID-C9BDED)
Middle Bronze Age (*c.* 1500–1300 BC)
Length: 169 mm Width: 64.2 mm Thickness: 31.4 mm Weight: 440.6 g
Brewood and Coven, Staffordshire

Palstaves are the most common axe used in the Middle Bronze Age and most are part of the Acton Park and Taunton metalwork assemblages. They differ from earlier flanged axes and Continental winged axes (*Lappenbeile*) in that they have a marked, often very deep stop ridge between the blade and the haft, like this example from Brewood and Coven, Staffordshire (WMID-C9BDED, Fig. 50). This is to stop the split wooden handle from slipping forward during the chopping motion. The term 'palstave' derives from the Icelandic *paalstab*, which was the term chosen by nineteenth-century Danish archaeologists for this type of axe because of its resemblance to a contemporary digging tool. The term *paalstab* became popular with nineteenth-century Scandinavian and German archaeologists and was, though reluctantly, also adopted by British scholars.

Palstaves were made in two-piece moulds, such as the two examples found near Hempnall, Norfolk (SF-2D55E2). Some palstaves have side loops and they are generally sparsely decorated, like our example from Staffordshire. The two moulds from Norfolk were used to make palstaves with a shield-shaped moulding below the stop ridge (hence their type name 'shield-pattern palstave'). Shield-pattern palstaves were part of the hoard from Halesworth, Suffolk (SF-13C7A2, Fig. 52). This hoard, as well as the hoard from the Usk area, Monmouthshire (NMGW-39F32D, Fig. 46), contain contemporary objects that palstaves could be associated with when found in hoards: side-looped spearheads, dirks and decorative objects linked with the Middle Bronze Age 'Ornament Horizon', such as gold strips, twisted torcs, Liss-type bracelets and Picardy-type related pins (see below).

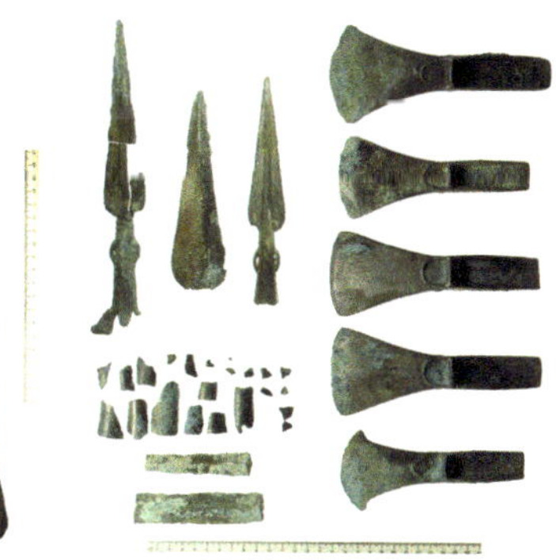

Above left: Fig. 50: Palstave from Brewood and Coven, Staffordshire (WMID-C9BDED).

Above middle: Fig. 51: A pair of two-piece moulds for casting palstaves from Hempnall, Norfolk (SF-Fig. 51: 2D55E2).

Above right: Fig. 52: Middle Bronze Age hoard including palstaves from Halesworth, Suffolk (SF-13C7A2).

17. Palstave adze (LEIC-916183)
Middle Bronze Age (*c.* 1500–1150 BC)
Length: 140 mm Width: 23 mm Thickness: 17 mm Weight: 159 g
Owston and Newbold, Leicestershire

Adzes or, owing to their close likeness to palstaves, commonly known as 'palstave adzes' are rare finds (Fig. 53). In contrast to palstaves, their body and blade sections are both long and slender and, unlike any other axe type, their blades are turned at a 90-degree angle, so not aligned with the blade. Although they have not been recorded in association with any other Age objects, they are generally considered to be of Middle Bronze Age date, primarily because they look so similar to palstaves (see No. 15). So far, only ten palstave adzes have been recorded on the PAS database. Their distribution appears to focus on the Midlands and the north-west, with specimens found in Cumbria (Crosby Ravensworth, LANCUM-5CE338, Fig. 54), Lancashire (Gisburn, LANCUM-64B7A7, and Horton, LANCUM-697908), Warwickshire (Tanworth-in-Arden, WAW-F2B395, Fig. 55) and Leicestershire (Swithland, LEIC-58C955, and Owston and Newbold, LEIC-916183, Fig. 53).

Above left: Fig. 53: Palstave adze from Owston and Newbold, Leicestershire (LEIC-916183).

Above middle: Fig. 54: Palstave adze from Crosby Ravensworth, Cumbria (LANCUM-5CE338).

Above right: Fig. 55: Palstave adze fragment from Tanworth-in-Arden, Warwickshire (WAW-F2B395).

18. Socketed axe of Type Taunton-Hademarschen (DEV-8D4931)
Middle Bronze Age (*c.* 1400–1150 BC)
Length: 121.55 mm Width: 30.4 mm Thickness: 30.5 mm Weight: 185.68 g
Otterton, Devon

Socketed axes of Type Taunton-Hademarschen are the earliest regular type of socketed axe in Britain and the near Continent. Our British examples are very distinct from other (much later) socketed axes and are now recognised as a regional type with a distribution in south and south-west England. Like the featured example from Otterton, Devon (DEV-8D4931, Fig. 56), and another from Marlborough, Wiltshire (WILT-C4C954, Fig. 57A), they all share a square socket, a thin, elongated side loop and a long, narrow body whose sides taper to a very narrow, only very slightly splayed blade. Due to their narrow blades it is likely that these tools were actually used as chisels rather than chopping axes. If decorated, they display one or two tongue-shaped moulded ridges with, possibly, an indistinct multi-lobed element towards the end of the larger outer loop, as can be seen on the incomplete example from Milton Abbas, Dorset (DOR-4DC8EA, Fig. 57B). Generally, socketed axes date from the Late Bronze Age, but at Yarmouth, Isle of White (IOW-C48CB1), a socketed axe of Type Taunton-Hademarschen was associated with Middle Bronze Age palstaves underpinning their typologically suggestive much earlier Middle Bronze Age date (Fig. 58).

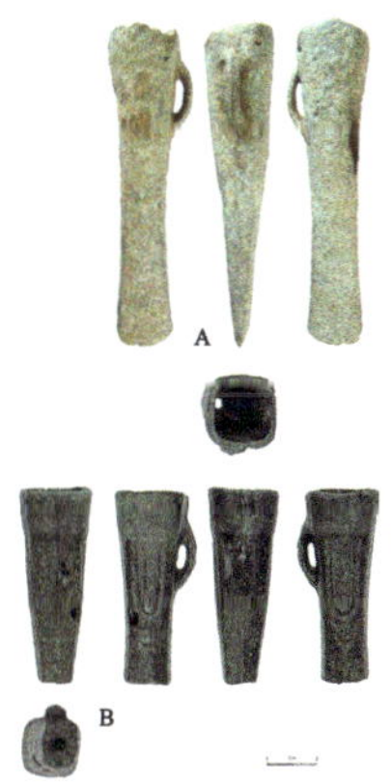

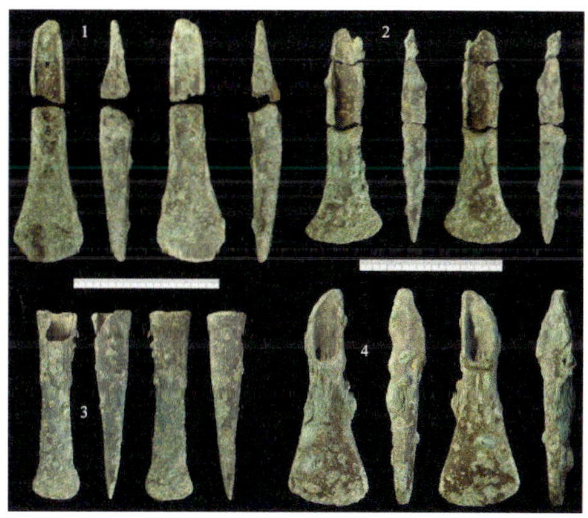

Above left: Fig. 56: Socketed axe of Type Taunton-Hademarschen from Otterton, Devon (DEV-8D4931).

Above middle: Fig. 57: Socketed axes of Type Taunton-Hademarschen from (A) Marlborough, Wiltshire (WILT-C4C954) and (B) Milton Abbas, Dorset (DOR-4DC8EA).

Above right: Fig. 58: Middle Bronze Age hoard from Yarmouth, Isle of Wight (IOW-C48CB1), containing three palstaves (Nos. 1, 2 and 4) and a socketed axe of Taunton-Hademarschen Type (No. 3).

19. Basal-looped spearhead (YORYM-7A5023)
Middle Bronze Age (*c.* 1400–1150 BC)
Length: 172.7 mm Width: 39.4 mm Weight: 191 g
Rylstone, North Yorkshire

Middle Bronze Age spearheads often had small moulded loops on the outside of the socket or at the base of the leaf- or flame-shaped blade, hence the use of the descriptive terms side-looped spearheads and basal-looped spearheads. Side-looped spearheads date slightly earlier (*c.* 1550–1300 BC) than basal-looped spearheads (*c.* 1400–1125 BC). A good example for a basal-looped spearhead is the example from Rylstone, North Yorkshire (YORYM-7A5023, Fig. 59), which survives in two large, joining fragments. It has a large leaf-shaped blade with loops incorporated into its base. Most of the outer edge of the blade is abraded, except around the tip where it is complete. The centre of the blade is divided by an expanding (tip to base) lozenge sectioned midrib. Conjoined at the base of the blade are two oval-shaped loops. When viewed in profile, the outer edges of the loops (loop plates) are lozenge shaped. A similar example with a differently moulded blade was recorded from Kingston Bagpuize with Southmoor in Oxfordshire (BERK-AAB536, Fig. 60). The other slightly earlier group of Middle Bronze Age spearheads, side-looped spearheads, have two small side loops on opposing sides of the socket, as can be seen in the examples from Wendlebury, Oxfordshire (OXON-838037, Fig. 61A), and from near Ely, Cambridgeshire (NMS-C64C06, Fig. 61B).

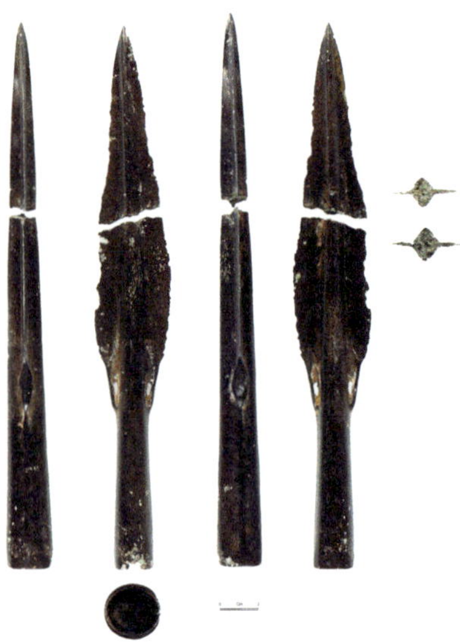

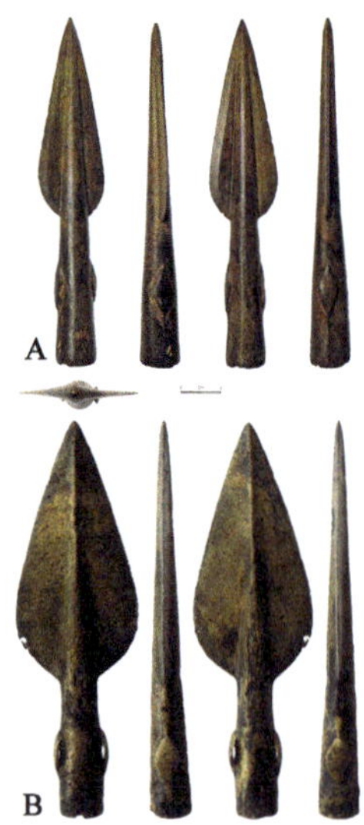

Above left: Fig. 59: Basal-looped spearhead from Rylstone, North Yorkshire (YORYM-7A5023).

Above middle: Fig. 60: Basal-looped spearhead from Kingston Bagpuize with Southmoor in Oxfordshire (BERK-AAB536).

Above right: Fig. 61: Two side-looped spearheads from (A) Wendlebury, Oxfordshire (OXON-838037) and (B) near Ely, Cambridgeshire (NMS-C64C06).

20. Dirk (LIN-E5872D)
Middle Bronze Age (*c.* 1550–1350 BC)
Length: 158 mm Width: 44 mm Thickness: 4.68 mm Weight: 89.15 g
Cranwell, Brauncewell and Byand's Leap, Lincolnshire

Middle Bronze Age and early Late Bronze Age blades for stabbing or thrusting are generally called 'dirk' or 'rapier' (see No. 20). Historically, dirks and rapiers are not two distinctive groups. An arbitrary length, 300 mm, was chosen to divide them. This was done on the basis that blades shorter than 300 mm could have been very versatile, possibly fulfilling a wider range of functions while blades longer than 300 mm were more specifically intended as thrusting weapons. Thus, bladed implements above 300 mm length are classed as 'rapiers' and bladed implements below 300 mm length are classed as 'dirks'. This distinction works well for complete or near-complete objects such as the dirks from Cranwell, Brauncewell and Byard's Leap, Lincolnshire (LIN-E5872D, Fig. 62), and Dalton, North Yorkshire (DUR-88691D), but it does not work for blade fragments without any defining features. Dirks had organic hilts that were kept in place with usually two small rivets, which are sometimes still in place, for example on the dirks from Nercwys, Flintshire (LVPL-55F121, Fig. 63B), and Blewbury, Oxfordshire (BERK-2C1328, Fig. 63A). On the latter, residue from the organic hilt remains around one of the rivets, suggesting that the dirk was deposited complete. In addition to these relatively common objects, there

Fig. 62: Dirk from Cranwell, Braucewell and Byard's Leap Lincs (LIN-E5872D).

is also a very rare group of six ceremonial dirks, which are much longer than 300 mm. Two have been recorded from the UK, which were found in Norfolk, one on a farm in East Rudham (NMS-C7EEF3, Fig. 64), the other near Oxborough. These dirks are massive, very heavy and have an intentionally blunted edge. They do not have any rivet holes suggesting that they were never intended to have a hilt. The other four examples were found in north-west continental Europe: Plougrescant (Brittany, France), Beaune (Burgundy, France) and Ommerschans and Jutphaas (Netherlands).

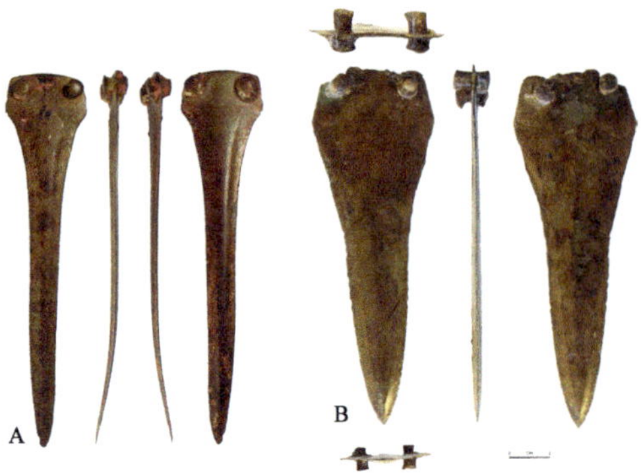

Left: Fig. 63: Two dirks from (A) Blewbury, Oxfordshire (BERK-2C1328) and (B) Nercwys, Flintshire (LVPL-55F121).

Below: Fig. 64: The massive ceremonial dirk discovered near East Rudham, Norfolk (NMS-C7EEF3).

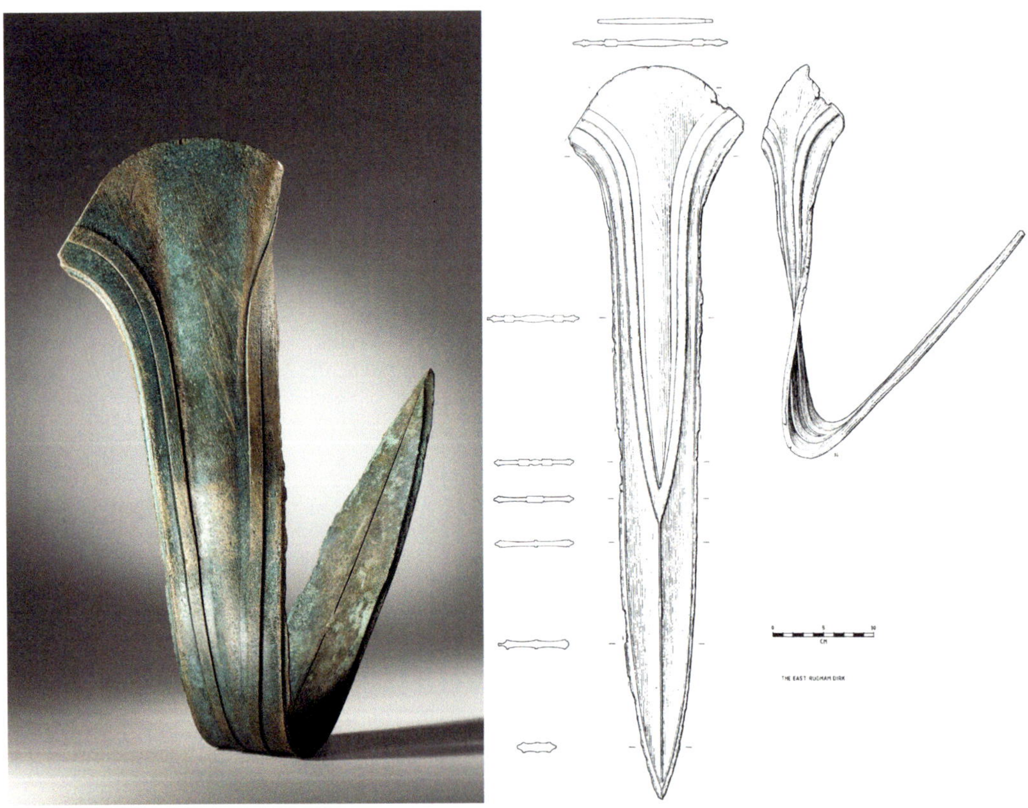

21. Rapier (SWYOR-7A4C37)
Middle Bronze Age (*c.* 1300–1125 BC)
Length: 345 mm Width: 38.7 mm Thickness: 5.56 mm Weight: 159 g
Hackforth, North Yorkshire

Due to their generally thin, narrow blades and overall lengths rapiers are rarely found complete; only three are recorded with the Portable Antiquities Scheme, for example from Hackforth, North Yorkshire (SWYOR-7A4C37, Fig. 65). They were found at Nettlestone and Seaview, Isle of Wight (IOW-D28401, Fig. 66A), and Bampton and Northmoor, Oxfordshire (SUR-5AE176 and LON-47F5C3). Incidentally the findspots are near rivers or in wetlands, liminal places that are often favoured for Bronze Age metalwork deposition. Two further discoveries, a hoard of two rapiers from Shillingstone, Dorset (WILT-8CBFA4, Fig. 67) and a single rapier from the River Alyn, near Wrexham (HESH-4CD185, Fig. 66B) were broken up into smaller pieces and/or bent before deposition. In contrast to these few complete finds, there is a great number of blade fragments recorded with the Portable Antiquities Scheme: including the entries where an identification was attempted, there are nearly 3,000 entries. However, blade fragments are extremely difficult to identify with absolutely certainty as having come from a dagger, a dirk, a rapier or a sword. Traditionally rapier blades are understood to have been much narrower than sword or dirk blades, but since their typologies are based mainly on the overall length of the weapons and, to some extent, on the shape of the hilt and number of rivets, blade fragments could have come from any of those bladed weapons.

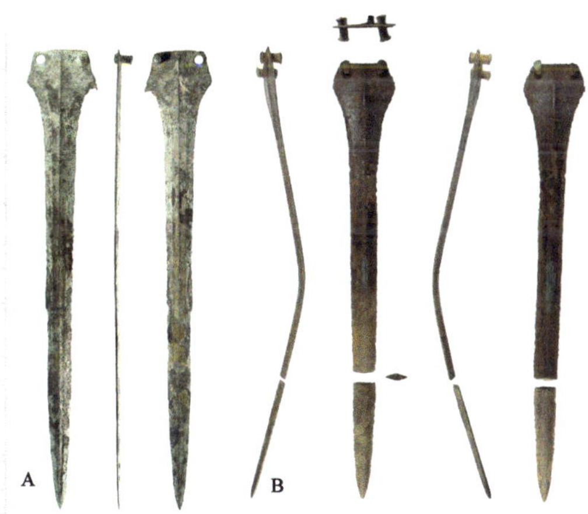

Above left: Fig. 65: Rapier from Hackforth, North Yorkshire (SWYOR-7A4C37).

Above middle: Fig. 66: Two rapiers from (A) Nettlestone and Seaview, Isle of Wight (IOW-D28401) and (B) River Alyn, near Wrexham (HESH-4CD185).

Above right: Fig. 67: Hoard of two broken up rapiers (A and B) from Shillingstone, Dorset (WILT-8CBFA4). The rivets (C) were also found in association with the blade fragments. They are very similar to Early Bronze Age dagger rivets (see Fig. 10), but found in association with certain blades, it is possible to date them.

22. Ceramic vessels (SF-9DAF03)
Middle Bronze Age (*c.* 1600–1200 BC)
Length: 37.23 mm Width: 45.59 mm Thickness: 5.58 mm Weight: 10.45 g
Near East Bergholt, Suffolk

Bronze Age pottery is rarely recovered and recorded as chance finds. Generally, Bronze Age pottery is very brittle and due to its earthy colours it can easily be overlooked by both metal detectorists and less experiences field walkers. However, occasionally a sherd is discovered and recorded. If enough of the vessel's original decoration or treatment survives, it could even be identified as a local ware, such as happened with this fragment that was found near East Bergholt, Suffolk (SF-9DAF03, Fig. 68). It is a rim sherd from a handmade vessel, made from a typically soft fabric with flint and grog temper. It was fired grey at the core but its surface is orange/brown on both outside and inside. Remarkably, on the outside, it retains an applied horseshoe-shaped moulding, which identifies it as part of the Ardleigh-style pottery tradition of north Essex.

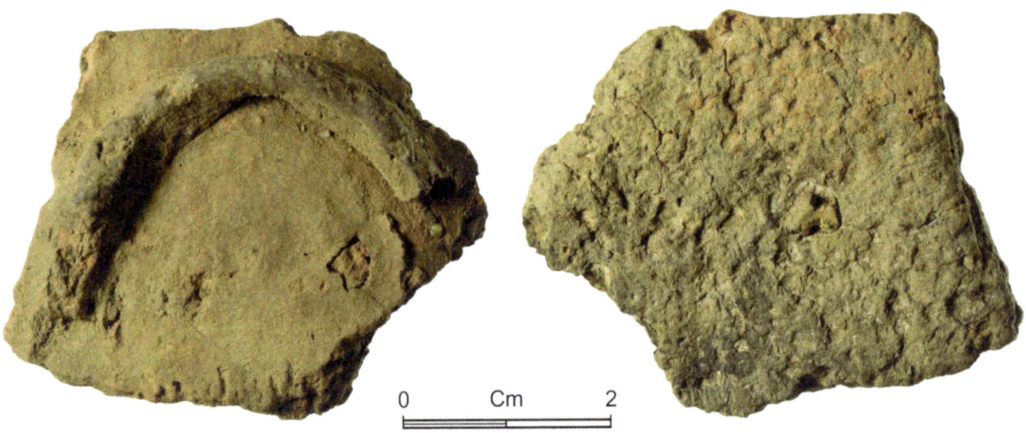

Fig. 68: Ceramic vessel fragment from East Bergholt, Suffolk (SF-9DAF03).

Chapter 6
The Ornament Horizon (*c.* 1400–1250 BC)

The so-called 'Ornament Horizon' describes part of the British Middle Bronze Age Taunton metalwork assemblage (*c.*1400–1250 BC). It is marked by the widespread occurrence of bronze and gold personal ornaments (Fig. 69), which are much rarer in the succeeding Later Bronze Age when personal ornaments and items made from gold are very rarely deposited in hoards. The personal ornaments of the 'Ornament Horizon' include objects such as pins, finger rings, arm-rings or bracelets and neck or body ornaments, which at the time were deposited alongside more well-established range of tools and weapons, such as palstaves, side-looped spearheads and rapiers (see above). The Ornament Horizon is prevalent in southern England, East Anglia and along the English/Welsh border; it is, however, almost unnoticeable in northern England and Scotland.

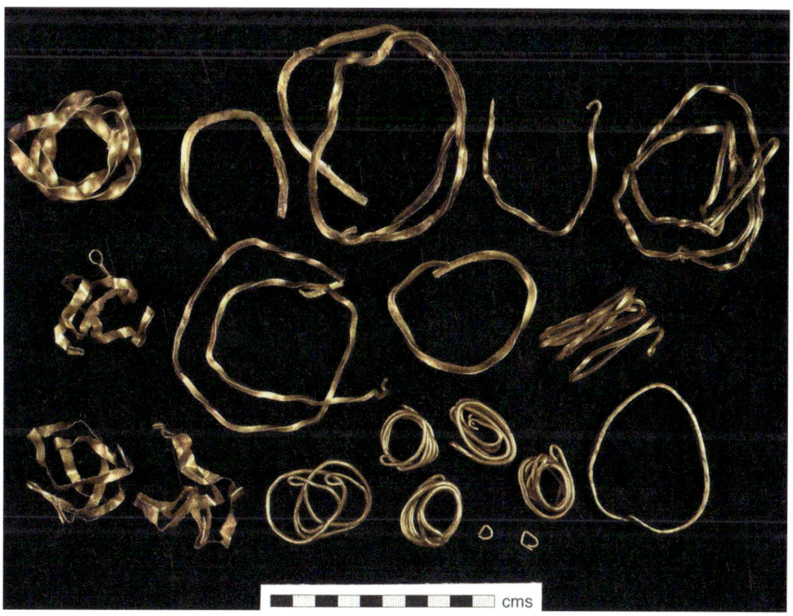

Fig. 69: Hoard of gold ornaments (arm-ring and neck ring coils) from Priddy, Somerset (SOM-1C2C53).

23. Ring (NMS-ACBFA4)
Middle Bronze Age (*c.* 1300–1150 BC)
Diameter: 15 mm Width: 8.5 mm Thickness: 1.5 mm Weight: 3.8 g
Fincham, Norfolk

Rings of any description are typical components of Middle Bronze Age assemblages of the Ornament Horizon. Occasionally, these rings are nondescript and undecorated and therefore difficult to identify if found on their own, such as this group of either spiral or 'stacked/fused' rings, which may have been all-purpose ring used as finger rings, hair ornaments or even ferrules. Composite penannular rings formed from C-sectioned, D-sectioned or sub-circular strips or bars are a well-known Middle Bronze Age artefact type as single finds or forming part of sets of linked rings. This gold example from Fincham, Norfolk (NMS-ACBFA4, Fig. 70), is a composite ring formed from three D-sectioned strips of gold, which were probably soldered together. These gold examples are probably related to bronze spiral rings of similar size, like the examples found near Axbridge, Somerset (SOM-36B525, Fig. 71A), and at Gisburn, Lancashire (LANCUM-A4E905, Fig. 71B). Individual finds of gold or bronze spiral or 'stacked' rings are extremely difficult to date exactly, but a Middle Bronze Age date is very likely because of the parallels from the Near Lewes Hoard (Sussex, see No. 26) and Horton (near Windsor, BERK-A5FFE5, Fig. 72)

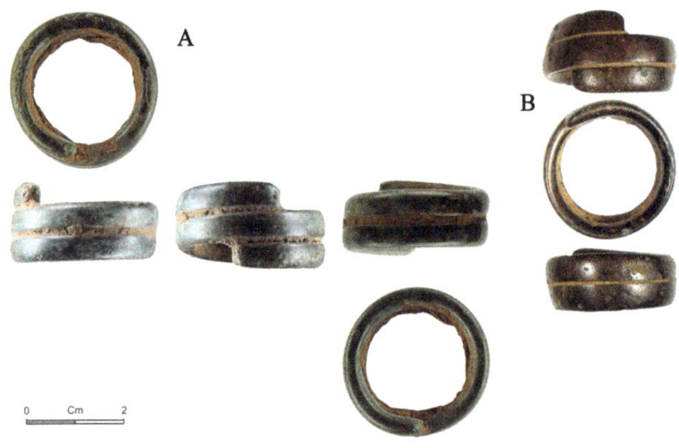

Above left: Fig. 70: Finger ring from Fincham, Norfolk (NMS-ACBFA4).

Above right: Fig. 71: Two coiled finger rings from (A) Axbridge, Somerset (SOM-36B525) and (B) Gisburn, Lancashire (LANCUM-A4E905).

Left: Fig. 72: Hoard of gold rings from Horton, near Windsor (BERK-A5FFE5).

24. Twisted torc/neckring (CAM-E5D871)
Middle Bronze Age (c. 1300–1150 BC)
Circumference (external): 1265 mm (excluding the terminals) Diameter (body): *c.* 9–10 mm Width of 'arms' of cruciform cross-section: *c.* 1 mm Weight: 732.4 g
East Cambridgeshire

The Middle Bronze Age Ornament Horizon in southern England is also characterised by the appearance of certain types of gold or bronze 'torcs', neck or body rings, such as this large example from East Cambridgeshire, made from gold (CAM-E5D871, Fig.73). It is a so-called four-flange twisted bar torc, which was made of three separate components: two very similar, undecorated, bent-back, 'trumpet'-shaped terminals, which were affixed to either end of an exceptionally long spiral twisted bar with very regular cruciform (i.e. '+' shaped) cross-section. The twisted torc from East Cambridgeshire is one of the few complete examples recorded with the Portable Antiquities Scheme, with other, more curled up specimens found as part of the Crowdown Hoard (West Berkshire, BERK-683F91, Fig. 2). However, fragments are known from Swanbourne, Buckinghamshire (BH-7128EA,

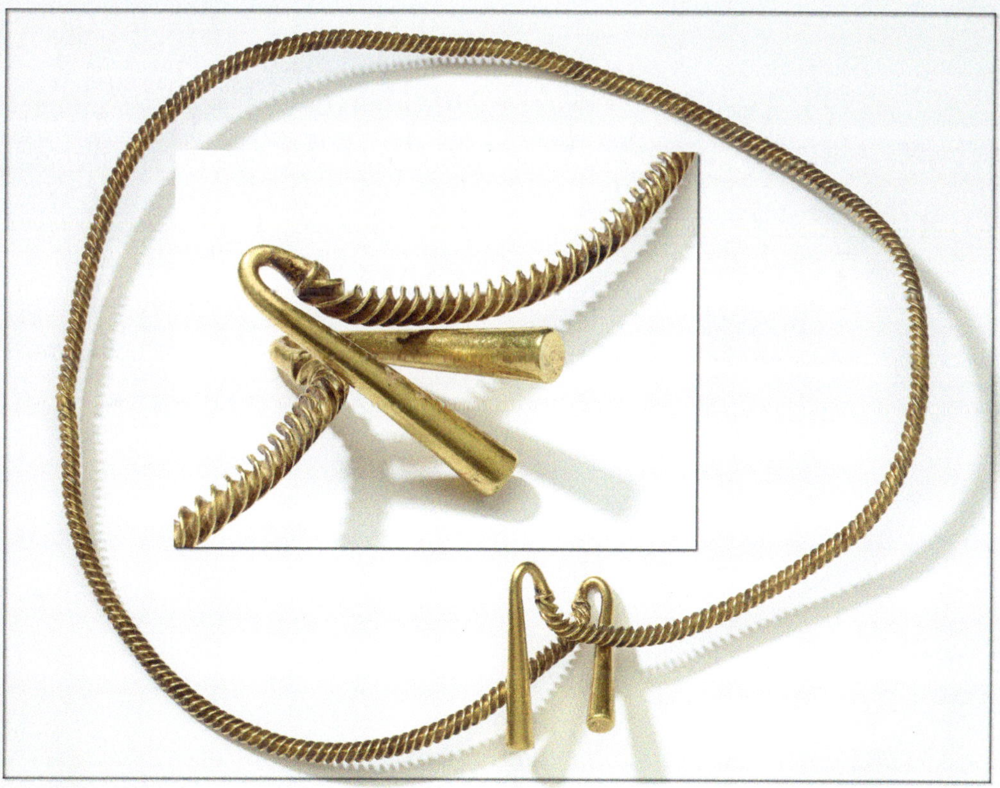

Fig. 73: Twisted gold body ring from East Cambridgeshire (CAM-E5D871). Inset: Close-up of the terminals.

Fig. 74A and B), Shorwell, Isle of Wight (IOW-CoCo54, Fig. 74C, and Swanmore, Hampshire (HAMP-DBAD3A, Fig. 74D). None of the bronze examples is as large as the twisted torc from East Cambridgeshire; they generally appear much stiffer, with a square rather than cross- ('+')shaped cross section, like the torc recorded from near Warminster, Wiltshire (WILT-12B9D2, Fig.75).

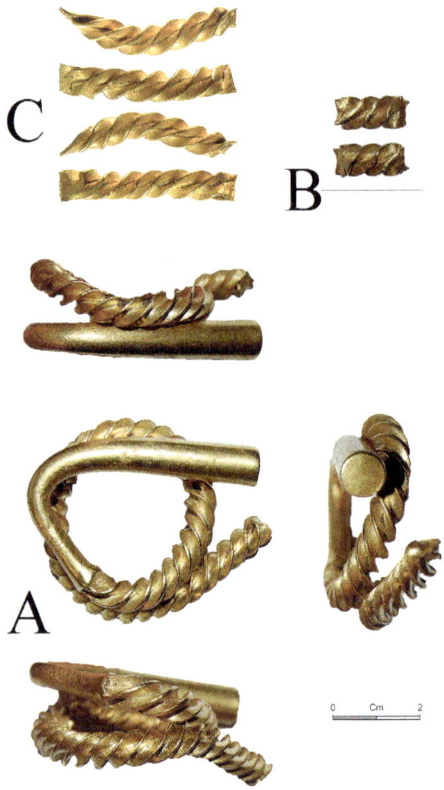

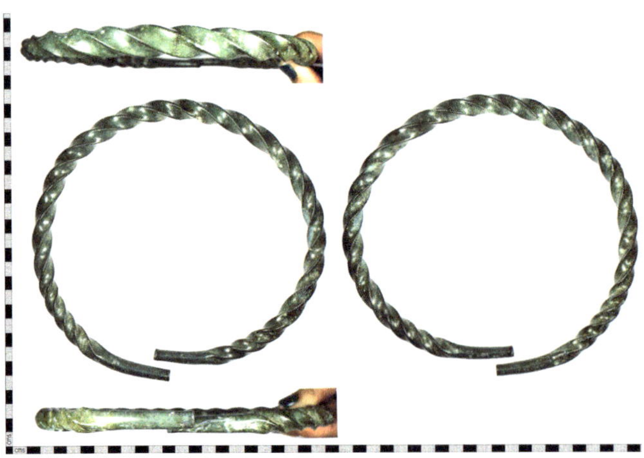

Above: Fig. 74: Four fragments of twisted gold rings from (A/B) Swanbourne, Buckinghamshire (BH-7128EA), (C) Shorwell, Isle of Wight (IOW-CoCo54) and (D) Swanmore, Hampshire (HAMP-DBAD3A).

Left: Fig. 75: Bronze twisted neck ring from Warminster, Wiltshire (WILT-12B9D2).

25. Bracelet/armring (FASW-DA4387)
Middle Bronze Age (*c.* 1300–1150 BC)
Diameter (external): 85 mm Diameter (internal): 60 mm Thickness: 18 mm
Stroud, Hampshire

In addition to smaller spiral rings and neck rings, the Southern British Ornament Horizon also includes flat or twisted arm-rings and bracelets, such as found in the Wylye Hoard (Wiltshire WILT-038191 2012T786, Fig. 77) and decorated bracelets of Liss type such as this example from Stroud, Hampshire (FASW-DA4387, Fig. 76). Liss-type bracelets are characterised by incised geometrical decoration. The example from Stroud is decorated with zig-zags made up of three or four lines with dotted borders divided by wide bands of cross-hatching. There is a cord motif on the lower edge with a row of dots above it. Liss-type bracelets also occur in hoards, for example at Portchester West (Fig. 77) and Hurstbourne Priors, Hampshire (HAMP-4B38A6 and SUR-590F5D). While Liss-type bracelets were made from bronze, other types of Middle Bronze Age bracelets were made from flattened strips of gold with hooked terminals, like these examples from Freshwater, Isle of Wight (IOW-0195D2, Fig. 78B) and the group of bracelets found near Woolaston, Gloucestershire (GLO-E9EC16, Fig. 78A).

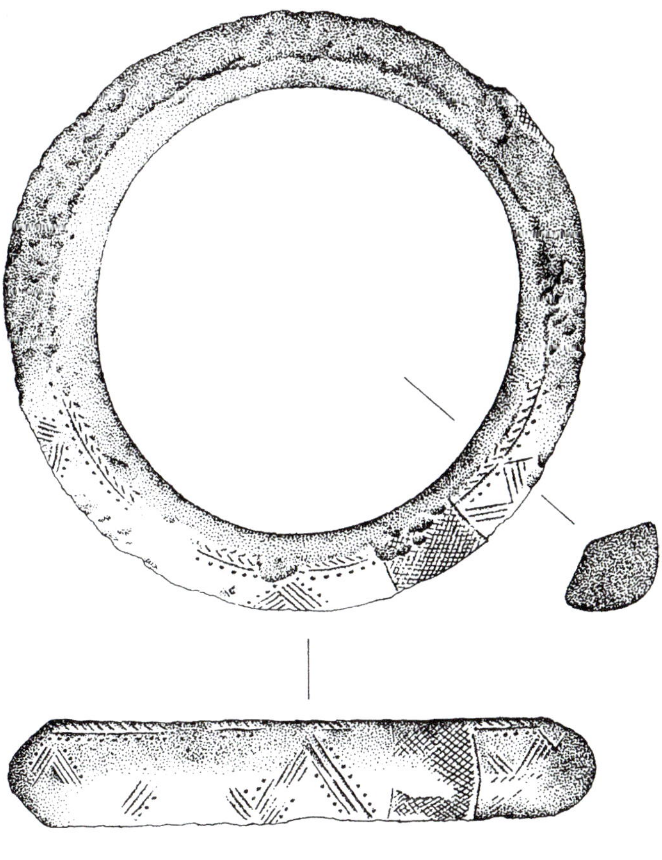

Fig. 76: A decorated arm-ring of Liss type from Stroud, Hampshire (FASW-DA4387).

Above: Fig. 77: Two hoards containing arm-rings. Above: The Portchester West Hoard, Hampshire (HAMP4B38A6). Below (not to scale): The Wylye Hoard, Wiltshire (WILT-038191/2012T786).

Left: Fig. 78: Gold armrings. (A) A group of bracelets found near Woolaston (Gloucestershire, GLO-E9EC16), and (B, inset) a fragment from Freshwater, Isle of Wight (IOW-0195D2).

26. Sussex Loop (SUSS-103D66)
Middle Bronze Age (*c.* 1400–1150 BC)
Length: 86.47 mm Width: 45.1 mm Thickness: 10.16 mm Weight: 69.28 g
Upper Beeding, West Sussex

'Sussex Loops' are a specific type of Middle Bronze Age bracelet known mainly from the Sussex area – hence the name. They have a very distinctive shape that makes it possible to attribute even fragments to this type, like this example from Upper Beeding, near Brighton (West Sussex, SUSS-103D66, Fig. 79). Complete Sussex Loops were found in the hoards from Ockam (Surrey, SUR-B41DB6) and Near Lewes (East Sussex, SUSS-C5D042, Fig. 80). Each Sussex Loop is made from one single rod with either circular, square or diamond-shaped cross section and tapering ends. The rod was bent in half with the 'folded end' made into a large oval or teardrop-shaped loop. The central sections of the two halves of the folded rod then ran parallel, forming the 'bracelet hoop' presumably around the wrist or arm, with the two rod terminals then curled around the centre apex of the loop. In hoards, Sussex Loops are associated with palstaves, pins, spiral rings and other ornaments.

Right: Fig. 79: Sussex Loop fragment from Upper Beeding, West Sussex (SUSS103D66).

Below: Fig. 80: The Near Lewes Hoard, Sussex (SUSS-C5D042), which contains, among other items, Sussex Loops, palstaves, a twisted neck ring, a quoit headed pin fragment and gold ornaments.

27. Pin (SUR-9D1663)
Middle Bronze Age (*c.* 1400–1250 BC)
Length: 74.85 mm Diameter: 24.75 mm Weight: 27.82 g
Near Witney, West Oxfordshire

The Middle Bronze Age is also known for the production of beautifully decorated pins, which may have been used as dress or hair pins, depending on their length. There are several recurring types, such as Picardy pins, quoit-headed pins and disc-headed pins, all of which occur in plain forms or with incised geometrical decoration and small side loops. This pin from near Witney (West Oxfordshire, SUR-9D1663, Fig. 81) is highly unusual in that it is extensively decorated and topped with a large circular head. The outer face of the circular head is a cylindrical projection with a dished interior; this is presumably intended for a missing setting, perhaps of amber. Around this cylinder is a circle of fourteen truncated cones, which project a little beyond the central cylinder. This highly unusual pin has no close parallels, but it is possibly related to Picardy pins, which are similarly decorated with a smaller head, like this example from Freckenham (Suffolk, SF-109C22, Fig. 82). Picardy pins are known from both British and Continental contexts and most examples are decorated and looped, though plain examples with central perforations are also known. One example, from Clanfield (Oxfordshire, SUR-1EFCC6: Fig. 83A), has a flat disc head that may have been the setting for a gem or inlay, and instead of a loop it has a pierced prominent projection in the form of an elongated diamond. Another common Middle Bronze Age pin type are quoit-headed pins, such as this example from Kingston Bagpuize (Oxfordshire, BERK-B33BF2, Fig. 83B). Quoit-headed pins are characterised by a ring head that sits centrally on the shaft (as opposed to Early Iron Age ring-headed pins where the top part of the shaft itself is bent into a ring). The ring is often flat and rarely decorated, but while all the other pins are smaller in size, quoit-headed pins come in a variety of sizes, some as long as 200–300 mm (for example, from Hopton-on-Sea and Marham, Norfolk, PAS-E40226 and NMS-3D6677). They may also occur in Middle Bronze Age hoards of the Ornament Horizon, for example from Hopton-on-Sea (Norfolk) and Portchester West (Hampshire, see No. 25, Fig. 78).

Fig. 81: A pin from Witney, West Oxfordshire (SUR-9D1663).

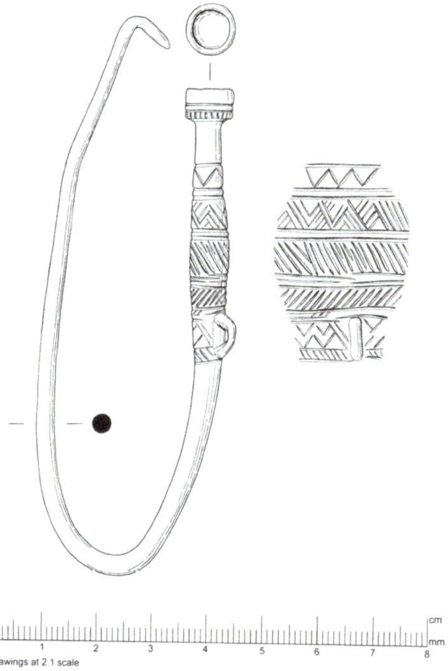

Right: Fig. 82: Picardy Pin from Freckenham, Suffolk (SF-109C22).

Below: Fig. 83: (A) A Picardy Pin from Clanfield, Oxfordshire (SUR-1EFCC6), and (B) a quoit headed pin from Kingston Bagpuize, Oxfordshire (BERK-B33BF2).

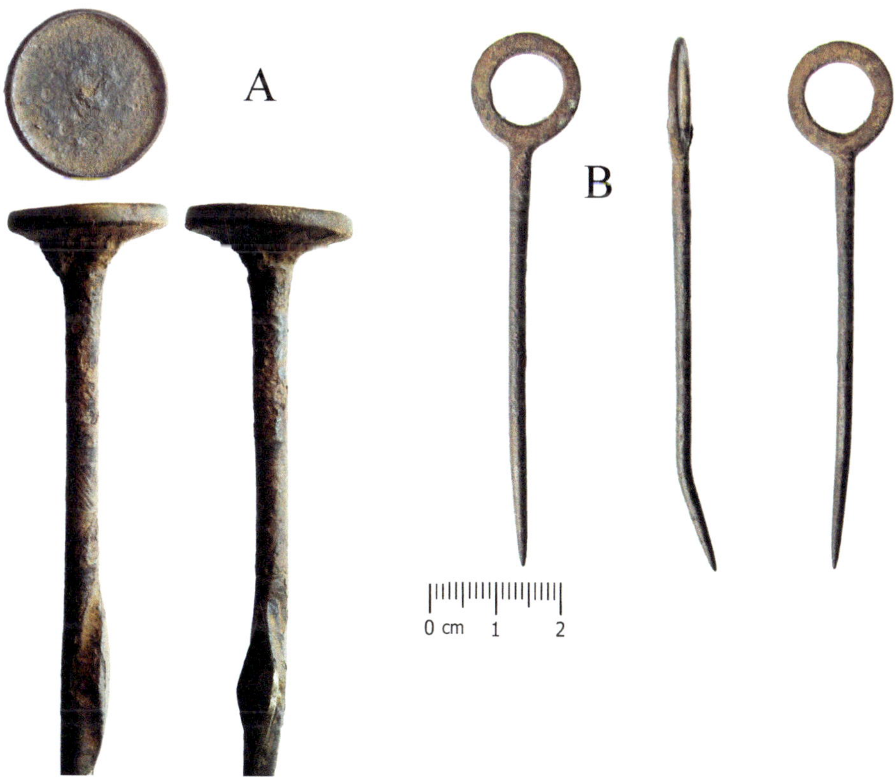

28. Bead/pendant (GLO-46CA05/2014T358)
Middle Bronze Age (*c.* 1300–1150 BC)
Height: 4.5 mm Weight: 0.45 g Diameter: 10 mm
Newent, Gloucestershire

Gold and bronze beads and pendants are another typical component of Middle Bronze Age assemblages of the Ornament Horizon. Like spiral rings and bracelet fragments, they can be difficult to identify and date precisely if found on their own. However, occasionally beads and pendants are found in hoards, such as in the beautiful hoard from Burton (Wrexham, PAS-5B1745, Fig. 85), which also includes a twisted gold torc, palstaves and gold stacked rings (see Nos 16, 23 and 24). A single hollow gold bead just like the four beads found at Burton was discovered not far from Newent (Gloucestershire, GLO-46CA05, Fig. 84) and there is crescent-shaped pendant made from wire from Arundel (Sussex, SUSS-4C1150/2005T421, Fig. 86A), which is remarkably similar to the pendant from Burton (Fig. 85 inset). The smaller beads are usually plain, hollow cast and have a biconical profile, while the pendants were made from tightly wound gold wire, with a soldered-on wire loop in the centre for suspension. A different kind of bead – more tubular in appearance and, potentially, made from a reworked bracelet section was recorded from Coberley (Gloucestershire, GLO-F8F3B7/2012T382, Fig. 86B).

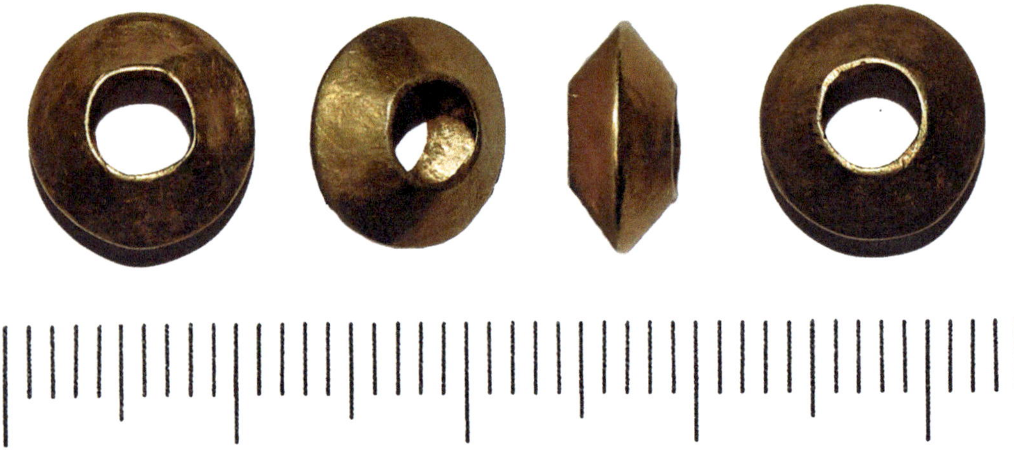

Fig. 84: A gold bead from Newent, Gloucestershire (GLO-46CA05).

Fig. 85: The Burton Hoard, Wrexham (PAS-5B1745). Inset, upper left: Close-up of the gold pendant.

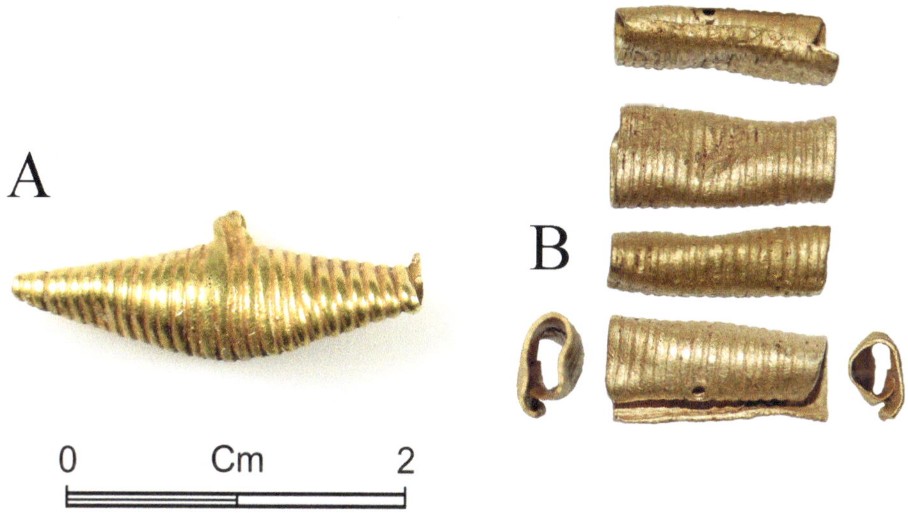

Fig. 86: Two different gold beads from (A) Arundel, West Sussex (SUSS-4C1150) and (B) Coberley, Gloucestershire (GLO-F8F3B7).

Chapter 7
The Late Bronze Age (*c.* 1000–800 BC)

The Late Bronze Age in Britain is predominantly characterised by the large-scale deposition of metalwork hoards (Fig. 87). They are extremely common in Yorkshire, South Wales and, especially, East Anglia and Kent. They are often made up of broken up fragments of tools and weapons and sometimes include ingots and waste metal such as casting jets. This leads to their general interpretation as either 'wholesale dumping' or 'recycling caches'. Much of the metalwork in circulation in the Late Bronze Age was not produced from fresh copper alloy but made from recycled Middle Bronze Age and earlier Late Bronze Age material, making the mining for ores less urgent. The deposition of so much metalwork in the Late Bronze Age was often considered to be a sign for disorder or aggression, but there is little else in the archaeological record to support that theory. Few burials survive and most of the excavated settlements indicate a mainly peaceful transition from the Late Bronze Age to the Early Iron Age.

In comparison with the previous periods, the final phase of British Bronze Age goldworking includes a far wider range of objects types, manufactures and decorations. Bar-working and sheet-working techniques were still dominant, but new techniques, such as gold plating, inlaid, and the creation of objects with hollowed body, are recorded. People also combined different goldworking skills: repoussé, incised and punched decoration. The main decorative patterns were grooves, rows of dots, concentric circles, conical projections, concentric and filled triangles, chevrons, diamond patterns and cross-hatch patterns. The results of those goldworking techniques are mainly neck rings, pendants, a diverse range of bracelets, sleeve and dress fasteners, penannular rings and lock rings.

Fig. 87: The Late Bronze Age hoard from Colwinston, Vale of Glamorgan (NMGW-CD2C58).

29. Ceramic vessel (ESS-A4B5F4)
Late Bronze Age (*c.* 1000–800 BC)
Burnham-on-Crouch, Essex

Late Bronze Age vessels are very rarely discovered intact because the pottery is brittle and does not always survive well in the ground. If a vessel is found in association with two or more items of prehistoric metalwork, it, too, is potential treasure, and needs to be lifted with care. The hoard from Burnham-on-Crouch (Essex, ESS-A4B5F4) is such an example (Fig. 88). The vessel was block lifted before being deconstructed along fault lines in the lab to remove the metalwork that had been placed inside (Fig. 88A–D). The ceramic fabric has a black core, and a patchy red-brown outer wall with flint inclusions throughout. While wrapped in cling film, the vessel was X-rayed in plan and profile before the contents were removed. The X-ray produced a very clear image of the condition and structure of

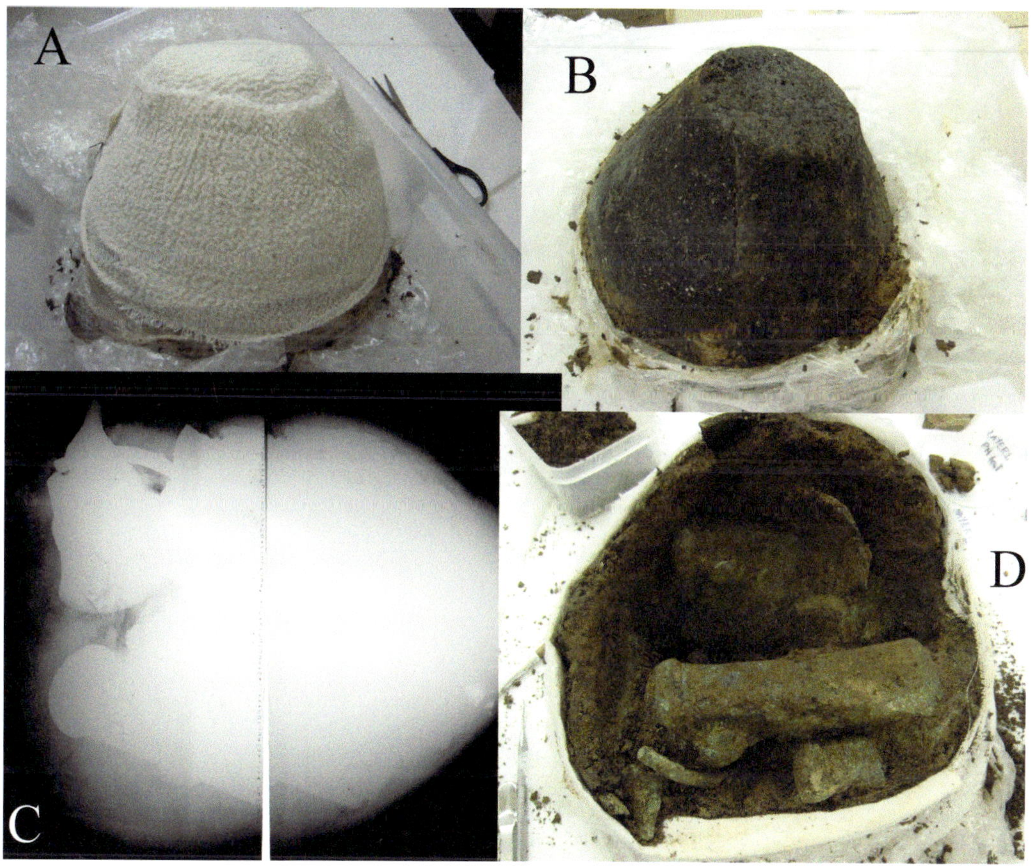

Fig. 88: The Late Bronze Age hoard from Burnham-on-Crouch, Essex (ESS-A4B5F4). A: The block-lifted ceramic vessel containing the hoard. B: Ceramic vessel prior to excavation in the lab (upside down). C: X-ray of the vessel; two socketed axes are on the left, towards the top of the vessel. D: During excavation in the lab.

the pot and it was used as a guide for the micro-excavation of the contents of the vessel. The top half of the pot was badly fractured with incomplete and shattered sides. Some side fragments were held in position by the metal contents. Individual artefacts were documented before being removed from the vessel.

The find from Essex is the only complete Late Bronze Age vessel recorded with the Portable Antiquities Scheme, but fragments of Earlier and Later Bronze Age pottery were recorded from Dereham (Norfolk, NMS-E126C2, Fig. 89C) and Keswick (Cumbria, LANCUM-477B84 and LANCUM-474FD0, Fig. 89A and B). An assemblage comparable to the Burnham-on-Crouch hoard is the earliest Iron Age hoard of socketed axes from Mylor (Cornwall, CORN-8FCBF5): thirty-three socketed axes were discovered in a complete vessel (Fig. 90).

Fig. 89: Late Bronze Age ceramic sherds from (A and B) Keswick, Cumbria (LANCUM-477B84 and LANCUM-474FD0) and (C) Dereham, Norfolk (NMS-E126C2).

Fig. 90: Early Iron Age ceramic vessel from Mylor, Cornwall (CORN-8FCBF5), which contained thirty-three socketed axes of Type Sompting, Variant Fig.heldean Down. (Photo: Laura Radcliffe)

30. Mould (LEIC-A6BB51)
Late Bronze Age (*c.* 1000–800 BC)
Mould: 1. Length: 151.04 mm Width: 63.92 mm 2. Length: 152.60 mm Width: 64.76 mm
Rothley, Leicestershire

Bronze two-piece moulds for casting Late Bronze Age socketed axes are not rare finds, although they are by no means common. They are often associated with other metalwork and seem to reassert the notion that Late Bronze Age hoards were buried by metalworkers or 'founders'. Examples of moulds from Late Bronze Age hoards come from Upton (Oxfordshire, BERK-56BD17, Fig. 92) and Rothley (Leicestershire, LEIC-A6BB51, Fig. 91). Both sets of moulds produced a different type of Late Bronze Age socketed axe. While the mould from Upton produced an axe of plain South-eastern type, the mould from Rothley produced a ribbed socketed axe of Type Welby. At Upton, the two mould halves were deposited together with three socketed axes that had been cast in them. Even though two different types of socketed axes were cast in the moulds from Upton and Rothley, the design of both sets of moulds is essentially the same. They both feature a tongue-and-groove design around the main axe impression, allowing the two pieces to be closely slotted together during casting. This can also be seen in a single find from Sutton (Suffolk, SF-839555, Fig. 93). The remains of a failed casting can be seen in the upper portion of one half of the Upton mould and this is now a pale white-yellow in colour.

Fig. 91: Two-piece mould from the Rothley Hoard, Leicestershire (LEIC-A6BB51).

Copper-alloy moulds for casting are also known from Middle Bronze Age contexts (e.g. from Hempnall, Norfolk (see No. 16) and Devizes (Wiltshire, WILT-FFC218). However, not all moulds were made from copper alloy; some were made from clay or stone, like the Late Bronze Age granite/pegmatite mould from St Keverne, Cornwall (CORN-031000, Fig. 93).

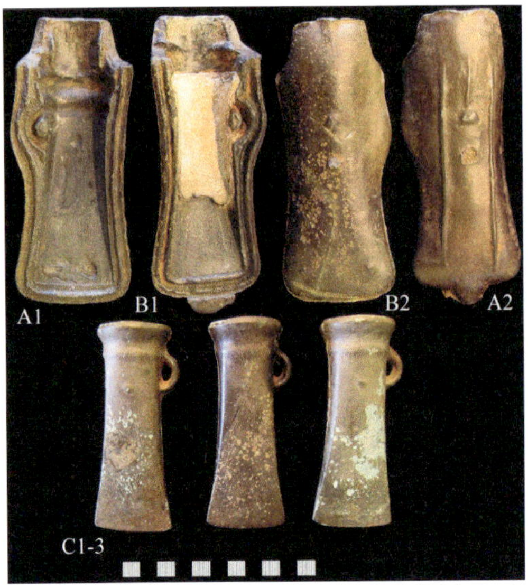

Fig. 92: Late Bronze Age hoard from Upton, Oxfordshire (BERK-56BD17), containing a two-piece mould and three socketed axes that were cast in the mould.

Fig. 93: Above: Late Bronze Age granite/ pegmatite mould fragment from St Keverne, Cornwall (CORN-031000). Below: Single mould half made from bronze found at Sutton, Suffolk (SF-839555).

31. Casting jet (IOW-CE75F0)
Late Bronze Age (*c.* 2150–800 BC)
Length: 26.7 mm Width: 29.9 mm Thickness: 19.0 mm Weight: 32.68 g
Freshwater, Isle of Wight

Late Bronze Age metalworking debris can be found singly or as part of hoards of metalwork. These objects are 'leftover' casting sprues or jets and complete for fragmented ingot 'cakes' (named after their shape). They are not finished objects in their own right but by-products from smelting and casting processes and were kept as ingots and potential recycling. A casting jet or sprue is the funnel-shaped bit at the top of the mould where the hot bronze was poured into the mould, and which was later broken off the cast object. A good example comes from the Isle of Wight (IOW-CE75F0, Fig. 94): the jet is roughly funnel shaped and in plan has a flat sub-oval concave head, the surface of which is irregular and pitted. This uneven surface was probably created when the molten metal was solidifying. On the underside there is a pair of sprue elements (feeders). Each feeder is in the form of a long stub, which is both turned inwards at the ends. The piece has a mid-dark green patina. It is possible that this casting jet is later than the Bronze Age. Similar casting jets have been recorded from Moulsford and Tetsworth (Oxfordshire, SUR-5168CC and BH-CC49D5, Fig. 95A and B) and a complete 'cake' ingot was found in Barnham (Kent, KENT-14DDA6, Fig. 96). The ingot is plano-convex in shape suggesting it was produced in a bowl furnace. The upper side is flat but with a large knop or swelling relating to the casting gate used in its production. The bottom is a rounded convex shape.

Fig. 94: A casting jet from Freshwater, Isle of Wight (IOW-CE75F0).

The ingot is heavily pitted likely due to a mix of impurities in its matrix and the uneven natural material used to create the bowl in which it was cast. The bowl furnaces were developed during the Mediterranean Bronze Age, becoming popular in Britain in the Late Bronze Age and were used intermittently to the modern era for many types of metal. It becomes much rarer in the production of copper alloy after the Roman period. Iron Age and Roman bun ingots tend to be much heavier than those of the Bronze Age, often weighing upwards of 12 kg. This example weighing only 1.25 kg would be suggestive of a Late Bronze Age date.

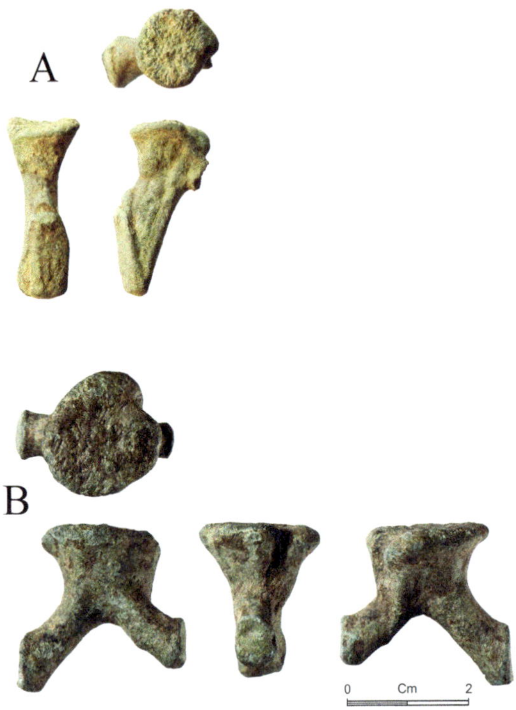

Left: Fig. 95: Two casting jets from Oxfordshire: (A) Moulsford (SUR-5168CC) and (B) Tetsworth (BH-CC49D5).

Below: Fig. 96: A complete 'cake' ingot from Barnham, Kent (KENT-14DDA6).

32. Socketed axe (DENO-8DB1B3)
Late Bronze Age (*c.* 1000–800 BC)
Length: 106.71 mm Width (Blade): 43.4 mm Weight: 302.7 g
Thoresby, Nottinghamshire

Axes are the most common Bronze Age object recorded with the PAS, and among this group socketed axes of the Late Bronze Age are by far the most numerous. They are found singly and in hoards, sometimes in very large numbers. Out of all Bronze Age artefacts recorded on the PAS database, socketed axes make up 10 per cent. They are sturdy, common objects that were used in almost every region in Britain. They are all of roughly the same shape and size, and slight regional differences are reflected in their different designs: we can, for example, distinguish South-eastern, Yorkshire and South Welsh type socketed axes. A very good example for a South-eastern socketed axe comes from Thoresby in Nottinghamshire (DENO-8DB1B3, Fig. 97B). Even though they were most widespread in south-east England (hence the name), they are found as far away as the south-west England and Scotland. The axe from Thoresby is a very typical example: it is undecorated, sub-rectangular in plan and triangular in profile, with a small side loop. A similar find comes from Stanton St John (Oxfordshire, BERK-2B2982, Fig. 99B). A different type of socketed axe, the Yorkshire type,

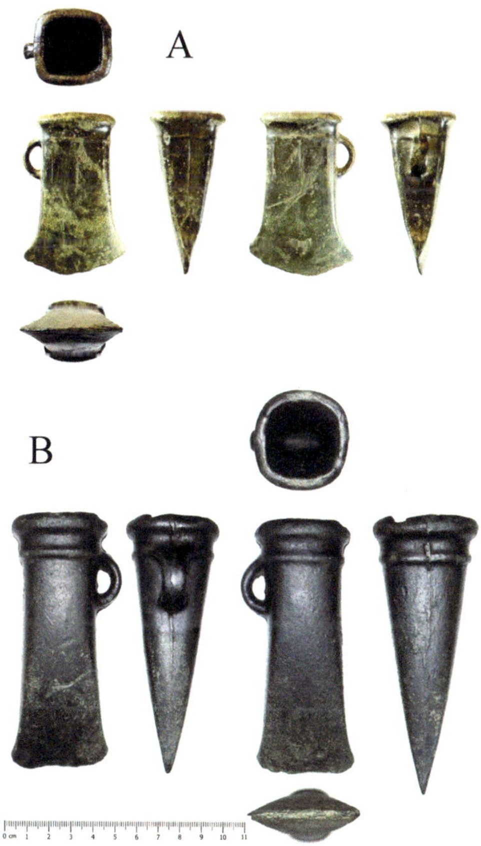

Fig. 97: A: One of a small hoard of two socketed axes from Stamford Bridge, Yorkshire (SWYOR-6EC462). B: A socketed axe of South-eastern type from Thoresby, Nottinghamshire (DENO-8DB1B3).

is somewhat shorter and decorated with three thin, widely spaced ribs, such as the two axes in the hoard from Stamford Bridge (Yorkshire, SWYOR-242536 and SWYOR-6EC462, Fig. 97A). A hoard found near Colwinston in the Vale of Glamorgan included a number of South Welsh axes (NMGW-CD2C58, Fig. 87). They are characterised by three ribs as well, but they are longer and often curved towards the centre of axe; also, the axes only have one flat mouth moulding. A faceted socketed axe and a rib-and-pellet decorated socketed axe were found in a small hoard from Eastbourne (Sussex, SUSS-8F5010, Fig. 1) and a ribbed South-eastern type axe (Fig. 98B) and a faceted axe of Meldreth type (Fig. 98A) were part of a small hoard from the Cotswolds (GLO-7577AB, Fig. 98). A very unusual type of socketed axe is the Ulleskelf type; Ulleskelf axes have two crescent-shaped indentations on either side of the body and a triple mouth moulding, as can be seen on the example from Benson (Oxfordshire, BERK-79C218, Fig. 99A).

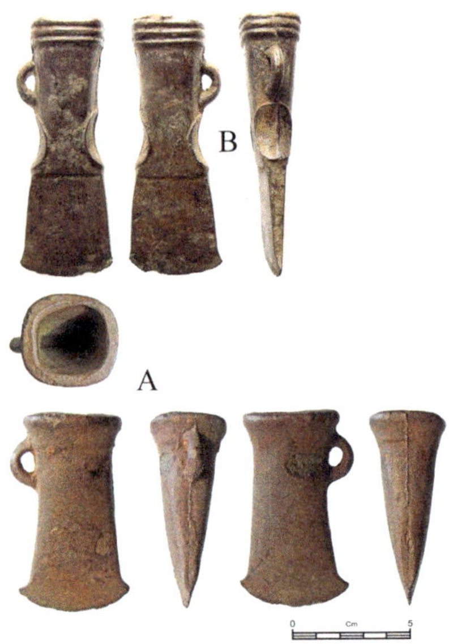

Above left: Fig. 98: Two socketed axes from a small hoard found in the Cotswolds, Gloucestershire (GLO-7577AB). A: Meldreth Type. B: Ribbed South-eastern type.

Above right: Fig. 99: Two socketed axes of different types from Oxfordshire. A: An Ulleskelf type axe from Benson (BERK-79C218). B: A plain South Eastern type from Stanton St John (BERK-2B2982).

33. Socketed gouge (NMS-523D79)
Late Bronze Age (*c.* 1000–800 BC)
Length: 84.5 mm Diameter: 17 mm
Horncastle, Lincolnshire

Socketed gouges are, like socketed axes and tanged chisels, very common Late Bronze Age tools. They are found singly or as part of hoards. Some earlier specimens are collared (e.g. Stinsford, Dorset, DOR-2A0940, Fig. 102A) and others, said to be slightly later in the Late Bronze Age (950–800 BC), have no collar, like the example form near Horncastle, Lincolnshire (NMS-523D79, Fig. 100), which also retains the remains of the wooden handle inside the socket. The socket is circular in section and tapers in the internal diameter. The opposite terminal, the blade edge, is 'C'-shaped in section. The blade is the terminal of an elongated triangular groove on the upper surface of the gouge. Generally, gouges display no decoration other than the occasional mouth moulding, but they can be different in size, length and the form of the 'C'-shaped blade, suggesting different gouges had different primary functions among woodworkers. Other examples are recorded from Ribbesford (Worcestershire, WAW-890416, Fig. 101) and Grendon (Warwickshire, WMID-41C97A). In hoards, socketed gouges often occur with tanged or socketed chisels or awls. The difference is that gouges have a curved blade and chisels have a straight blade (see No. 34), as can be seen in this slightly later Late Bronze/Early Iron Age transitional socketed chisel from Lenham in Kent (KENT-9E799C, Fig. 102B).

Above left: Fig. 100: Socketed gouge from near Horncastle, Lincolnshire (NMS-523D79).

Above middle: Fig. 101: Socketed gouge from Ribbesford, Worcestershire (WAW-890416).

Above right: Fig. 102: Socketed gouges from (A) Stinsford, Dorset (DOR-2A0940) and (B) Lenham, Kent (KENT-9E799C).

34. Tanged chisel or leather-working knife (BERK-4008DB)
Late Bronze Age (*c.* 1000–800 BC)
Length: 85.3 mm Width: 27.5 mm Diameter: 13.5 mm
Kingston Bagpuize, Oxfordshire

Apart from socketed axes and gouges, there are a number of other types of Late Bronze Age woodworking tools such as awls, knives and, one of the most common ones, tanged and collared chisels such as this example from Kingston Bagpuize, Oxfordshire (BERK-4008DB, Fig. 103). The chisel is in good condition and appears undamaged, with evidence for use wear on the blade tip and edge. The chisel has a tapering square-sectioned tang, which ends in a collared handle stop before it goes over into the flat triangular chisel blade. Similar chisels were recorded from Sanddown, (Isle of Wight, IOW-8EDC79, Fig. 104A), Ilam (Staffordshire, WMID-30DE52), Hordley (Shropshire, WREX-9F314E) and Well (North Yorkshire, DUR-5BADA1, Fig. 104B), but their general elongated shape, very thin blades and general resemblance to later Early Iron Age socketed leather-working knives suggest that they could have been leather-working rather than wood-working tools.

In addition to these flat chisels/knives there is a whole range of other artefacts that are most certainly part of the Late Bronze Age woodworking toolkit, for example socketed

Fig. 103: Tanged and collared chisel from Kingston Bagpuize, Oxfordshire (BERK-4008DB).

chisels like the ones from Bradborne (KENT-62F309, Fig. 105A) and Buckland Newton (Dorset, DOR-EE8574, Fig. 105C), the latter of which shows some rare decoration around the collar moulding. Furthermore, there are socketed tools with a shorter but sturdier blade from Highmoor (Oxfordshire, SUR-519C20), Barham (Kent, KENT-2A2156, Fig. 105B) and Swinfen (Staffordshire, WMID-E1B777).

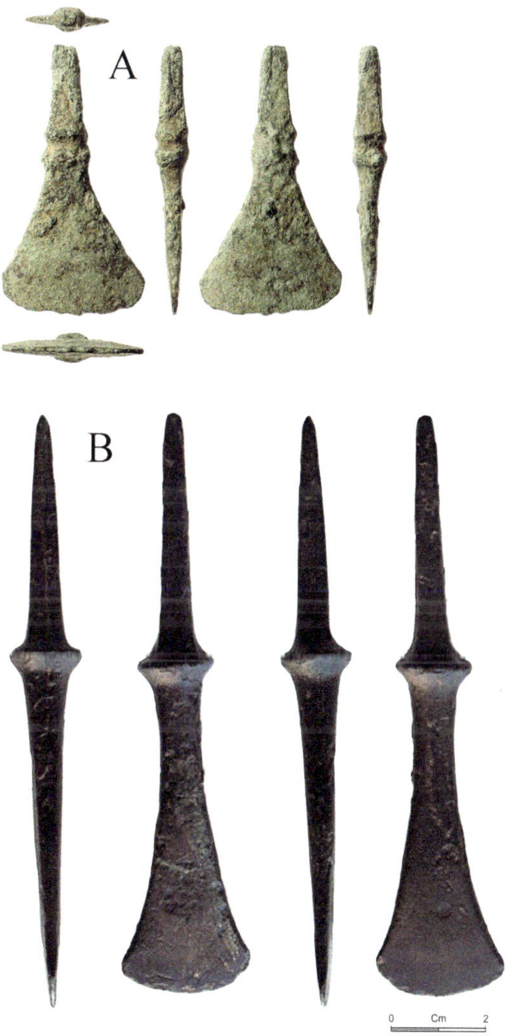

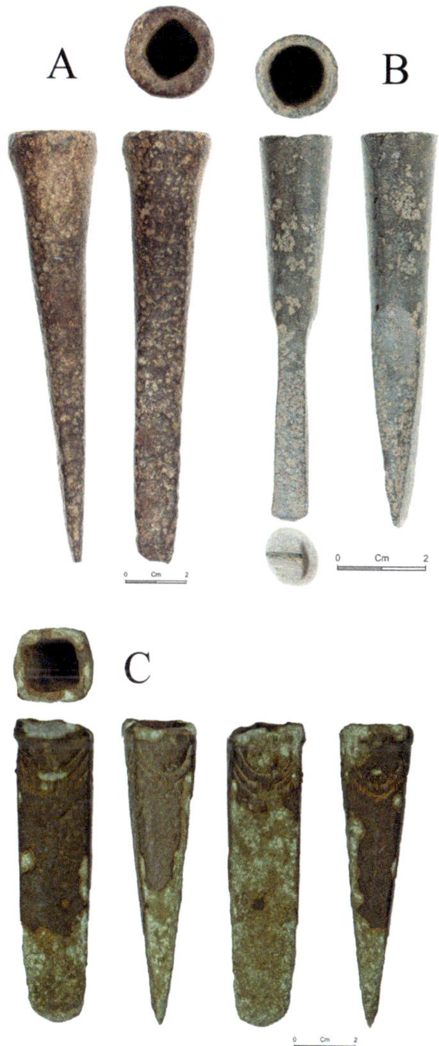

Above left: Fig. 104: Two tanged and collared chisels from (A) Sanddown, Isle of Wight (IOW-8EDC79) and (B) Well, North Yorkshire (DUR-5BADA1).

Above right: Fig. 105: Different types of woodworking tools. A: Socketed chisel from Bradborne, Kent (KENT-62F309). B: Socketed tool with a short, sturdy blade from Barham, Kent (KENT-2A2156). C: Decorated socketed chisel from Buckland Newton, Dorset (DOR-EE8574).

35. Bone awl (WILT-98DF4E)

Late Bronze Age (*c.* 1000–800 BC)
Length: 36.58 mm Width: 10.81 mm Thickness: 4.16 mm Weight: 6.48 g
Enford, Wiltshire

Another widespread tool type is the awl or point. In the later Middle and Late Bronze Age they were often made from copper alloy but there certainly were awls made from organic materials, too, such as this bone awl from Enford in Wiltshire (WILT-98DF4E, Fig. 106) – they just did not survive as well in the ground and are thus rare finds. In this example from Wiltshire one end of the bone retains the distal condyle while the other has been narrowed to create a pointed tip. The tip would have been used to pierce other materials. The front of the awl shows a lower recess, created by removing part of the bone, which reveals an inner chamber. The reverse part is smooth with a central incised line running down through it. The object has been filed and polished. This awl was found with a sherd of flint-tempered Late Bronze Age pottery recorded as WILT-99E11D, hence the certainty in date.

There are also awls made from bronze. However, they are often difficult to identify or date because, as with all tools, their general shape often does not change over the centuries. However, in later periods awls were more likely made from iron. The most typical Late Bronze Age forms are awls with or without collar or stop ridge, e.g. from Loggerheads (Staffordshire, WMID-7999D4, Fig. 107) without a collar and Kilham (East Riding of Yorkshire, YORYM-EEFF88, Fig. 108) with moulded collar or stop ridge, presumably to stop the awl being driven deeper into the organic handle when in use.

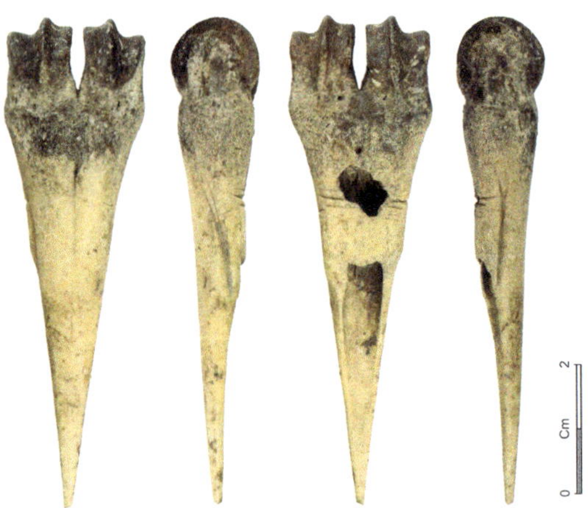

Above left: Fig. 106: A bone awl from Enford, Wiltshire (WILT-98DF4E).

Above middle: Fig. 107: Bronze awl from Loggerheads, Staffordshire (WMID-7999D4).

Above right: Fig. 108: Bronze tanged awl with stop ridge from Kilham, East Riding of Yorkshire (YORYM-EEFF88).

36. Socketed hammer (DUR-4E1468)

Late Bronze Age (*c.* 1000–800 BC)
Length: 76.56 mm Height: 24.28 mm Width: 20.35 mm Weight: 142 g
Gilmonby, County Durham

Socketed hammers are not as frequently reported as other Late Bronze Age metalworking tools, but they are not uncommon nevertheless. The most northerly reported example comes from Gilmonby, County Durham (DUR-4E1468, Fig. 109). It is sub-rectangular in cross-section and has casting seams along the sides indicating that it was cast in a two-part mould. The hammer tapers sharply from the socket toward the midpoint, before again flaring more gently toward the hammer face. The striking face of the hammer shows evidence of extensive use wear, with a pronounced uneven slant visible, together with numerous nicks. This hammer was part of a hoard (DUR-1F5057) that also includes sword and spearhead fragments and socketed axes. Other socketed hammers have been reported from near Stratford (Warwickshire, WAW-75FD95, Fig. 110A) and Kirkbymoorside (North Yorkshire, LVPL-89D1D3, Fig. 110B). Although occasionally found in the north and north-west, socketed hammers are much more common in East Anglia and southern England. Quite often they are plain and unassuming like this example from Amesbury, Berkshire (BERK-CA241B, Fig. 111A), but sometimes they are decorated with circular mouldings or a hanging triangle/chevron moulding like this example from Winsham (Somerset, SOM-D7BB09, Fig. 111B).

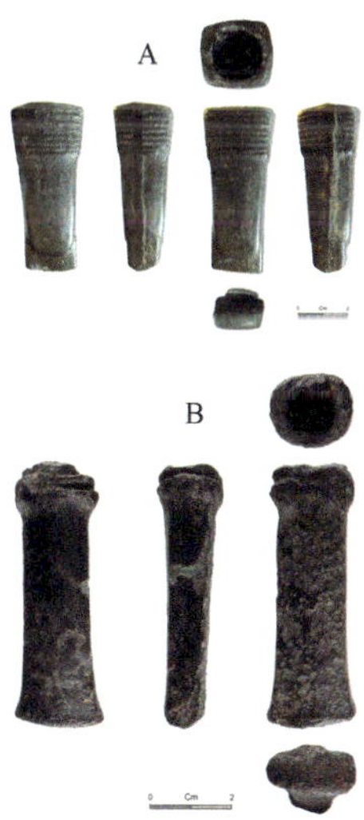

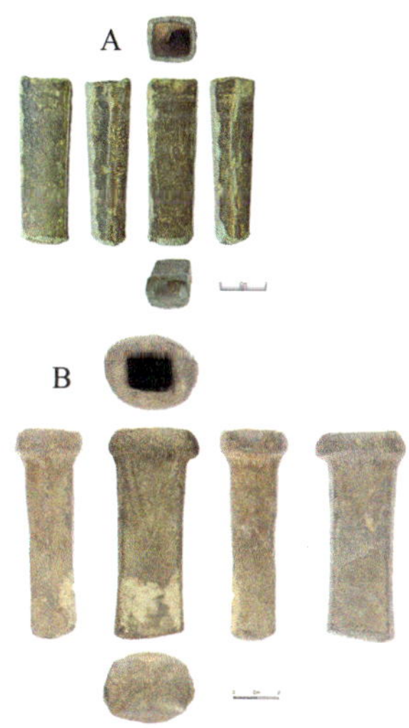

Above left: Fig. 109: A socketed hammer from Gilmonby, County Durham (DUR-4E1468).

Above middle: Fig. 110: Socketed hammers from (A) Stratford, Warwickshire (WAW-75FD95) and (B) Kirkbymoorside, North Yorkshire (LVPL-89D1D3).

Above right: Fig. 111: Socketed hammers from (A) Amesbury, Berkshire (BERK-CA241B) and (B) Winsham, Somerset (SOM-D7BB09).

37. Anvil (NMS-15E1DC)
Late Bronze Age (*c.* 1000–800 BC)
Length: 53.5 mm Thickness: 13 mm Weight: 43.44 g
Scarning, Norfolk

Copper-alloy anvils are rare but important finds and easily overlooked. There are only six Late Bronze Age examples recorded on the Portable Antiquities Scheme's database, the two most easily recognisable examples coming from Scarning (Norfork, NMS-15E1DC, Figs 112 and 113) and Elham (Kent, KENT-0278AC, Fig. 114). They are both beaked anvils with two beaks/spikes at right angles. On the example from Norfolk, however, the larger beak/spike is triangular openwork with a gabled work surface on the straight end. The other beak/spike is collared where it springs from one side of the broad end of the triangular beak, is oval-sectioned and tapers to a point. Like other Late Bronze Age tools, anvils are found both singly and as part of hoards.

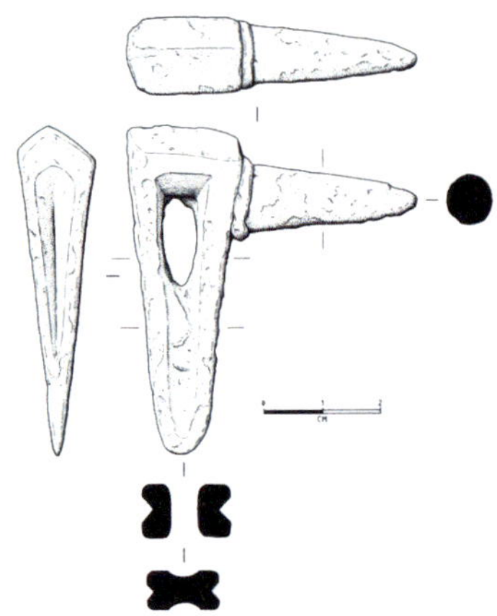

Above left: Fig. 112: A bronze anvil from Scarning (Norfork, NMS-15E1DC).

Above right: Fig. 113: Bronze anvil from Scarning, Norfork (NMS-15E1DC).

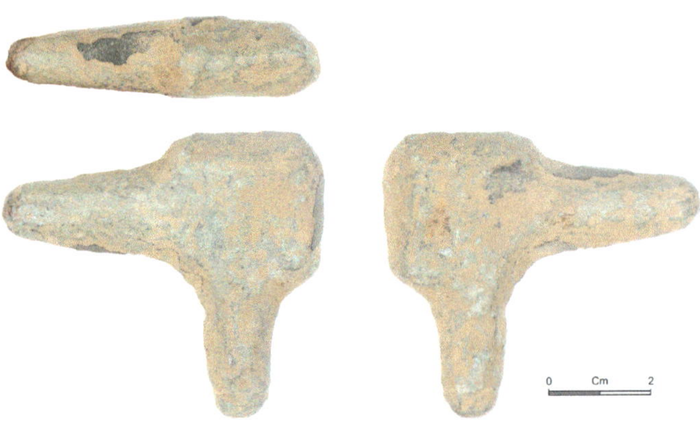

Fig. 114: Bronze anvil from Elham, Kent (KENT-0278AC).

38. Bugle-shaped object (ESS-A3EFF3)
Late Bronze Age (*c.* 1000–800 BC)
Length: 34.69 mm Weight: 25.03 g
Burnham-on-Crouch, Essex

While weapons and tools are common finds in Late Bronze Age contexts, smaller fitting and decorative objects are less common. These fittings and ornaments often do not have a straight-forward identification either and are named after their shape, i.e. bugle-shaped objects, buttons or rings. They are, supposedly, harness or cart fittings, or else belt buckles or buttons for clothing. One of the most common ones are the enigmatic so-called 'bugle'-shaped objects, like the one found at Harrietsham (Kent, KENT-E6C2B2, Fig. 116B). Bugle-shaped objects are also found in Late Bronze Age hoards in south-east England and northern France. They may be related to buckles or strap fittings such as the example from Burnham-on-Crouch (Essex, ESS-A3EFF3, Fig. 115). This is a hollow fitting with a zig-zag-shaped border similar to one found as part of a Late Bronze Age hoard from St Michael's Mount (Cornwall, CORN-A8B9A0). They are both hollow, with rectangular front and back plates, but the example from Essex is missing its buckle and its 'teeth' are turned outwards rather than inwards. The moulded ornament bar section, which resembles the bugle-shaped object from Kent with four teeth, is known from fragments in hoards such as Isleham, Cambridgeshire, and Cassiobridge Farm, Watford, Hertfordshire. Another slightly earlier Late Bronze Age object type commonly associated with horse harness are rings that resemble later Iron Age terrets, such as the example from Lavenham (Suffolk, ESS-B46EE5, Fig. 116A). The artefact can be closely paralleled to examples in the Late Bronze Age hoard from Parc-y-Meirch (Abergele, Conwy). This hoard comprises an incomplete harness set for two chariot ponies, which also includes small buttons with concentric mouldings, like the ones found at Great and Little Chishill (Cambridgeshire, BH-E9F0E9, Fig. 117) and Claverley (Shropshire, WMID-498A82, Fig. 117).

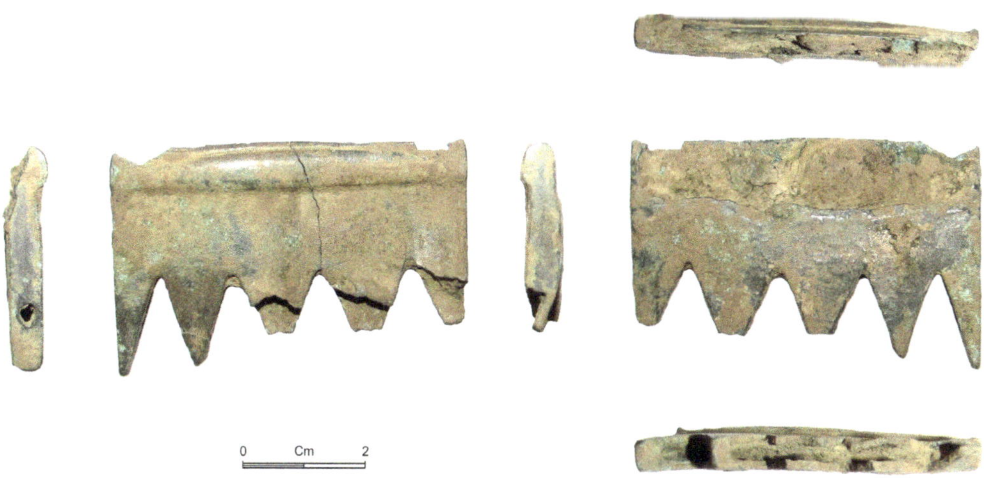

Fig. 115: Bugle-shaped mount or fitting from Burnham-on-Crouch (Essex, ESS-A3EFF3) – part of the Burnham-on-Crouch Hoard (Find No. 29).

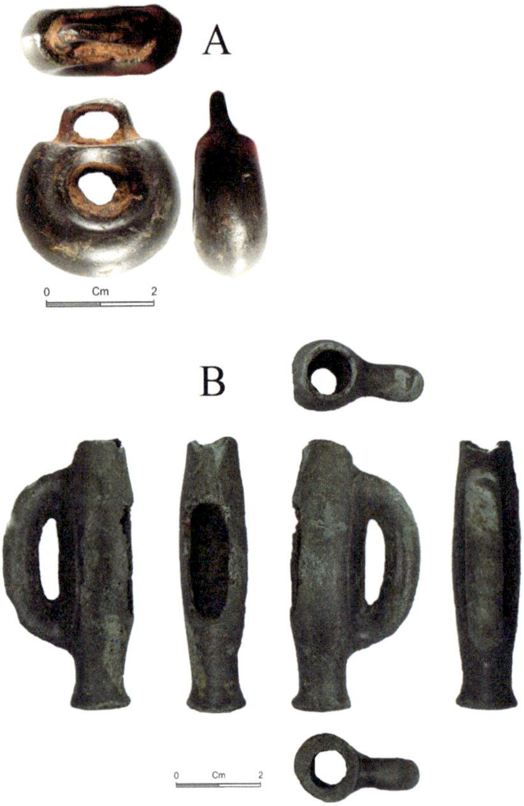

Fig. 116: Two different Late Bronze Age mounts. A: A small 'mini-terret' from Lavenham, Suffolk (ESS-B46EE5). B: A 'bugle-shaped' object from Harrietsham, Kent (KENT-E6C2B2).

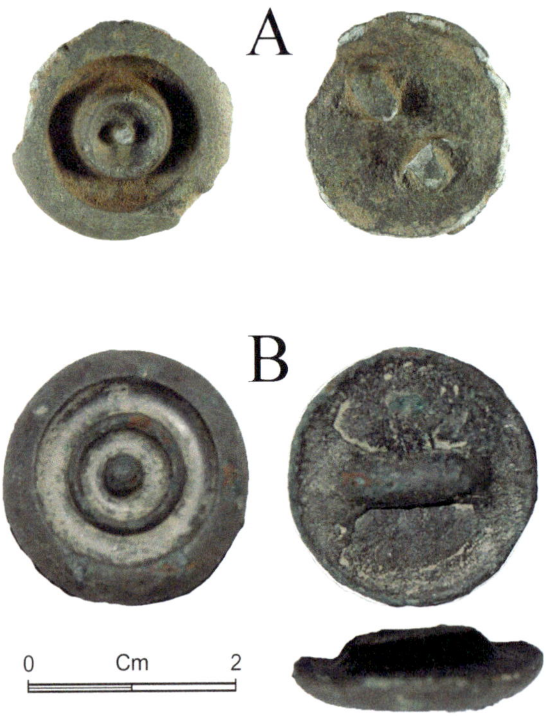

Fig. 117: Two 'buttons' from(A) Great and Little Chishill, Cambridgeshire (BH-E9F0E9), and (B) Claverley, Shropshire (WMID-498A82).

39. Knife (SWYOR-CAF110)
Late Bronze Age (*c.* 1000–800 BC)
Length: 75 mm Width: 23.5 mm Thickness: 13.17 mm Weight: 45.39 g
Norton, Doncaster

Socketed knives are another common Late Bronze Age find; they, too, occur on their own and, like the other tool types, in hoard contexts. They have a flat oval socket and a symmetrical blade and are often referred to as knives of Thorndon Type. In the specimens from Norton (Doncaster, SWYOR-CAF110, Fig.118) and Timsbury (Bath and North East Somerset, GLO-B7DA21, Fig. 119A), the blade has broken away from the socket but another, more complete (though very worn) example was recorded from Whitchurch (Warwickshire, SUR-5680D4, Fig. 119B). A knife from Willerby (North Yorkshire, DUR-850CB6, Fig. 119C) has a curved blade. This is very unusual and may suggest that the knife was used as a hook or scraper rather than a knife.

Among the corpus of Late Bronze Age bladed tools are also the so-called 'hog-back' knives or 'racloirs' (french: *scraper*). They are usually triangular in shape with a central perforation and three bevelled, sharpened edges, as in the examples from Bagillt (Flintshire, LVPL-F81A02, Fig. 120A) and Piddletrenthide (Dorset, SOMDOR-FFE225). Two other racloirs recorded

Fig. 118: Two joining fragments (socket and knife blade fragment) of a socketed knife from Norton, Doncaster (SWYOR-CAF110).

with the PAS are of crescent and flat trapezoidal shape with no central perforation, but they, too, are characterised by their sturdy appearance and sharp, bevelled edges all around. These examples come from Caerwent (Monmouthshire, NMGW-B18276, Fig.120B) and Winterbourne Steepleton (Dorset, SOMDOR-FFE225). The date for these scrapers or 'racloirs' appears to be long running, from Middle to Late Bronze Age, as a mould for a triangular example was found at Trevalga, Tintagel (Cornwall), in a Middle Bronze Age context dating to *c.*1400–1300 BC, but they are also known from Late Bronze Age hoards, e.g. Eaton (Norfolk).

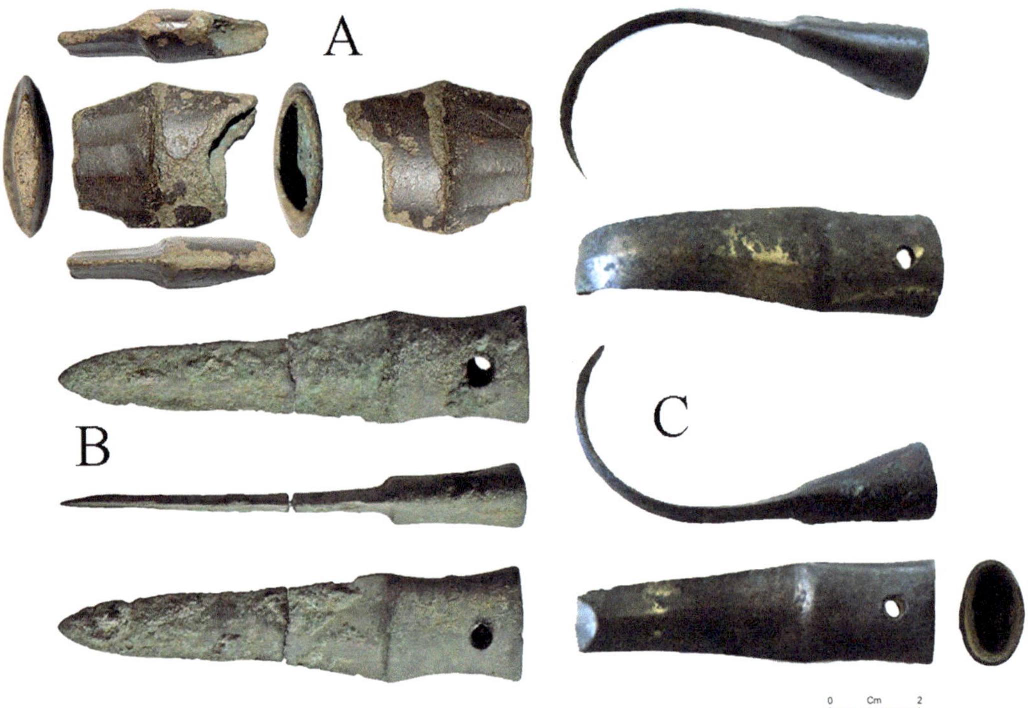

Above: Fig. 119: A: A socketed knife fragment from Timsbury, Bath and North East Somerset (GLO-B7DA21). B: an almost complete socketed knife from Whitchurch, Warwickshire (SUR-5680D4). C: A curved socketed knife from Willerby, North Yorkshire (DUR-850CB6).

Left: Fig. 120: Two Late Bronze Age knives. A: A triangular 'hog's-back knife' from Bagillt, Flintshire (LVPL-F81A020). B: A crescent-shaped knife from Caerwent, Monmouthshire (NMGW-B18276).

40. Sickle (SOM-4AE60B)
Late Bronze Age (*c.* 1600–800 BC)
Length: 66.6 mm Width: 18.2 mm Thickness: 4.5 mm Weight: 16.58 g
St Sampson, Cornwall

Bronze Age sickles are seldom found complete, but a number of blade fragments or potential blade fragments have been reported and recorded on the Portable Antiquities Scheme's database. Unless complete or almost complete, sickles fragments are very difficult to identify and date precisely. However, their blades differ from simple knife blades (see No. 39) in curvature and, potentially, an additional mid-rib. Often only the tips with part of the slightly curved blade are found, for example from St Sampson (Cornwall, SOM-4AE60B, Fig.121) and Tenterden (Kent, PUBLIC-653814, Fig. 122A). The latter example also displays the often typical thick, slightly curved midrib, common in Late Bronze Age and earliest Iron Age bronze sickles. The only complete Late Bronze Age sickle recorded on the Portable Antiquities Scheme's database is a sickle of a type virtually unknown in Britain; it is a sickle of typical Continental form, which was found at Welwyn (Hertfordshire, BH-6CC3F5, Fig. 123B). Unlike this sickle, which has a short hilt plate, our native British prehistoric sickles tend to have sockets or ring sockets, like a fragment that was part of the Burnham-on-Crouch hoard (Essex, ESS-3C3A75, Fig. 122B). The latest bronze sickles were long-lived and are also found in earliest Iron Age contexts, which is why the group of laterally socketed, 'heeled' sickles are generally dated to the Late Bronze Age/Early Iron Age transition. One complete example was recorded from Kingston Bagpuize (Oxfordshire, BERK-AC4A08, Fig. 123A).

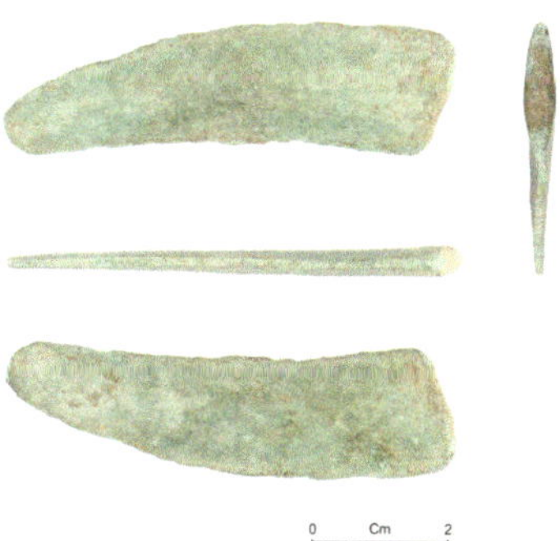

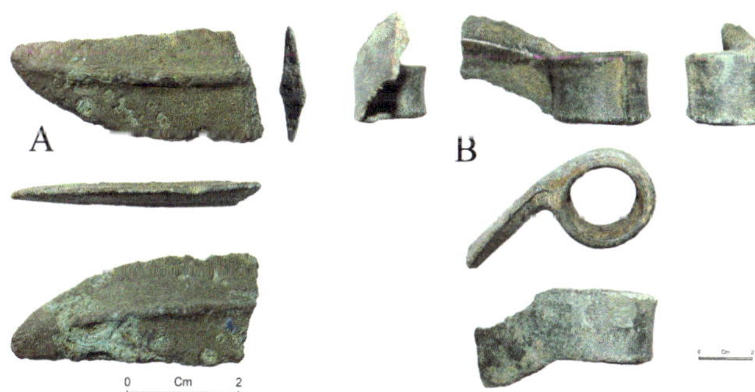

Above left: Fig. 121: Sickle blade fragment from St Sampson, Cornwall (SOM-4AE60B).

Above right: Fig. 122: Sickle fragments. A: Sickle blade tip from Tenterden, Kent (PUBLIC-653814). B: Ring sickle fragment from the Burnham-on-Crouch hoard, Essex (ESS-3C3A75).

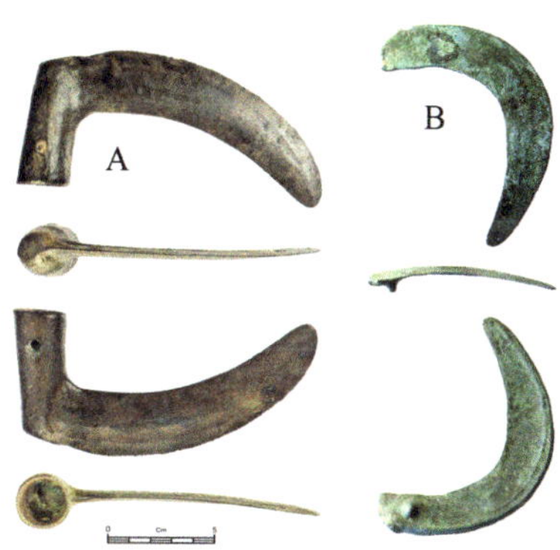

Right: Fig. 123: Complete sickles. A: A transitional Late Bronze/Early Iron sickle from Kingston Bagpuize, Oxfordshire (BERK-AC4A08). B: A Continental Late Bronze Age sickle from Welwyn, Hertfordshire (BH-6CC3F5).

41. Razor (CORN-D746F1)
Late Bronze Age (*c.* 1000–800 BC)
Length: 89 mm Width: 54 mm Thickness: 3 mm Weight: 28.9 g
Ely, Cambridgeshire

Among the corpus of Bronze Age bladed implements, razors are another common type. They are related to knives but have a tang rather than a socket for attaching an organic handle. The most common form of Late Bronze Age razor is the tanged bifid razor of Feltwell type, like the example found at Ely (Cambridgeshire, CORN-D746F1, Fig. 124). The word bifid describes that the blade was divided by a deep cleft or notch. The tang is decorated with six vertical grooves on one face and five grooves on the other, which are unevenly spaced and extend below a circular perforation to the tang. Type Feltwell razors are common in Scotland and England but rarer in in Wales and Ireland. A razor of slightly more unusual form was recorded from Bacton (Suffolk, SF-0FB985, Fig. 125). Its blade is leaf shaped with a lenticular cross-section and, even though badly damaged, it seems to have had a more elaborate handle, possibly a moulded openwork. The blade, however, is very similar to a group of plain tanged razors with a lenticular or leaf-shaped blade, examples of which were found at Barton Bendish (Norfolk, NMS-5BFE67, Fig. 126B) and Routh (East Yorkshire, YORYM-4525A3, Fig. 126A). The example from Routh has been folded over, but was originally of the same shape as the razor from Barton Bendish. These objects are recorded as razors, but they could also have been used as knives.

Above left: Fig. 124: Tanged bifid razor from Ely, Cambridgeshire (CORN-D746F1).

Above middle: Fig. 125: An unusual razor from Bacton, Suffolk (SF-0FB985). The razor would have had additional decorative rectangular castings around the handle section.

Above right: Fig. 126: Two plain tanged razors with lenticular shaped blades from (A) Routh, East Yorkshire (YORYM-4525A3) and (B) Barton Bendish, Norfolk (NMS-5BFE67).

42. Sword (HAMP-24C69E)
Late Bronze Age (*c.* 1000–800 BC)
Length: 556 mm Width: 48.2 mm Thickness: 9.5 mm Weight: 380 g
Romsey Extra, Hampshire

Chance discoveries of complete Late Bronze Age swords are as rare as chance discoveries of complete earlier Middle Bronze Age dirks and rapiers. The sword found at Romsey Extra (Hampshire, HAMP-24C69E, Fig. 127) is almost complete, but broken in two pieces. The hilt section is present, identifying it as a sword of Ewart Park type, similar to the fragment found at Marham (Norfolk, NMS-025B42, Fig. 128A). Before deposition, the sword from Romsey Extra had deliberately been bent into an elongated S-shape in profile and has

Above: Fig. 127: Two large joining sword fragments from Romsey Extra, Hampshire (HAMP-24C69E).

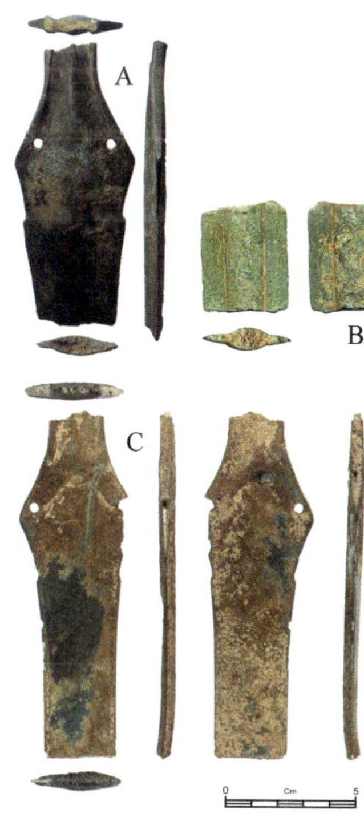

Right: Fig. 128: Three sword fragments from (A) Marham, Norfolk (NMS-025B42: Ewart Park Type), (B) West Knighton, Dorset (DOR-B4D511, fragment of Carp's Tongue sword blade), and (C) Skipton, North Yorkshire (YORYM-FFC826, Ewart Park Type, part of hoard).

broken at one of these bends. Another almost complete sword, from Madley (Herefordshire, GLO-37B31F), had been broken up in seven almost equal-sized fragments prior to deposition. The bending and breaking of swords prior to deposition was almost certainly intentional: the sword had to be heated to become plastic and was then struck with a hammer causing the breakage but also any other deformation, such as bending or twisting. Sword blade and hilt fragments are often components of metalwork hoards, for example at Tuxford (Nottinghamshire, PAS-1EB110) and Skipton (North Yorkshire, YORYM-FFC826, Fig. 128C). The sword fragments from Romsey Extra and Marham can be identified and dated because they are hilt fragments, but sometimes the blade sections are distinctive, too, as for example in Carp's Tongue and related sword types, which can be identified from a small blade section alone (West Knighton, Dorset, DOR-B4D511, Fig. 128B). The hilts of most swords are plates with rivet holes or slots to attach organic handle plates, but some swords were socketed (Great Moulton, Norfolk, NMS-4DE0A9, Fig. 129B). Very occasionally, fragments of Continental swords are discovered in British contexts, for example in the hoard from Cherry Burton (East Riding of Yorkshire, YORYM-958D05) and a single find from near Lewes (Sussex, SUSS-761CD0, Fig. 129A).

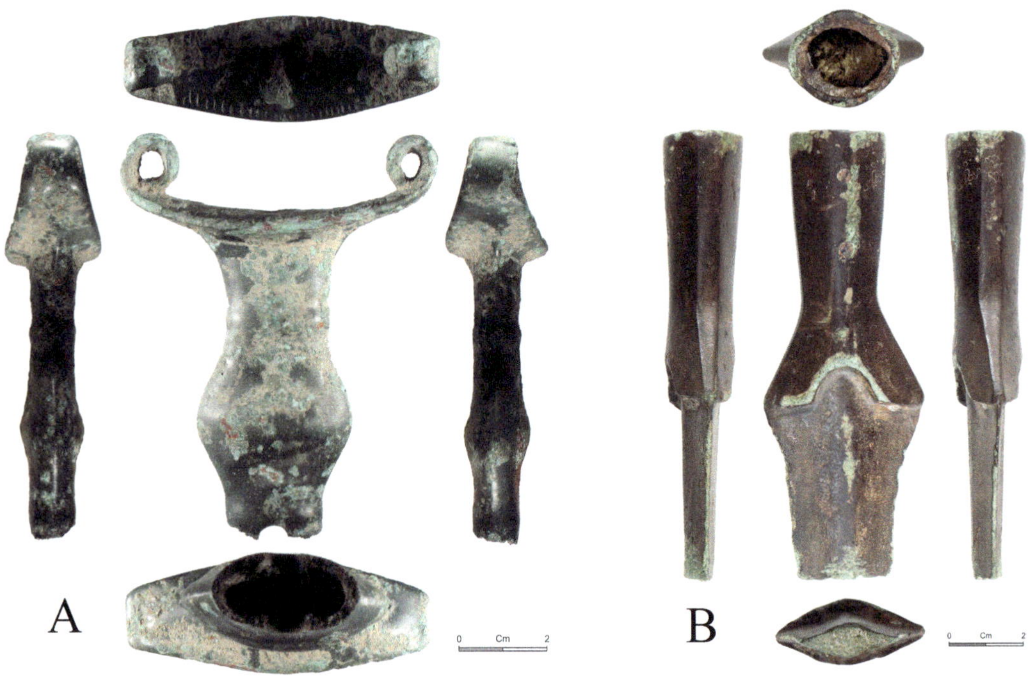

Fig. 129: Unusual sword handles from (A) near Lewes, Sussex (SUSS-761CD0, from a Continental Hallstatt sword) and (B) Great Moulton, Norfolk (NMS-4DE0A9, a socketed handle).

43. Spearhead (DOR-DC23F5)
Late Bronze Age (*c.* 1000–800 BC)
Length: 167.9 mm Width: 27.52 mm Thickness: 11.43 mm Weight: 69.07 g
Iwerne Minster, Dorset

Late Bronze Age spearheads are socketed and usually have a leaf-shaped blade. They often have two peg holes on opposing sides of the socket to attach the spearhead to a long wooden shaft. Large specimens may be barbed or hollow or have lunate openings in the blade, such as the example from Ufton Nervet (Berkshire, SUR-49AF85, Fig.132C). Like swords and axes, spearheads may be found singly and in hoards (e.g. Trevethin, Torfaen, NMGW-3EA2A8, Fig. 131). Some smaller spearheads are stumpy with wide sockets that may carry incised decoration around the opening. The spearhead from Iwerne Minster (Dorset, DOR-DC23F5, Fig. 130) probably dates to the very early Late Bronze Age because it still has a small side loop. It is a large specimen with complete leaf-shaped blade and a long, circular socket. It is undecorated, unlike the spearhead from Wallingford (Oxfordshire, BERK-FCF913, Fig. 132D), which is elaborately decorated with three sets of three incised lines around the circumference of the socket; the first row of three is located just above the mouth. The second set of lines is surmounted by punched decoration of two squares crowned by a triangle. This grouping of punched decoration is repeated around the circumference. The two peg holes are located within this band of decoration. Sometimes, a spearhead only survives with damage to the blade and socket, like on the example from Brearton (North Yorkshire, SWYOR-BB6C1F, Fig. 132A). Here, the damage stems from possible accidental nicks and corrosion, but on a spearhead found near Chilcomb (Hampshire, SUR-0FB443, Fig. 132B), the tip of a spear was clearly intentionally damaged prior to deposition. The spear has rounded edges and one side of the blade has seven deep nicks, which create seven 'barbs'. Normally, cuts and nicks along the blade edges are the result of combat damage or an intentional 'killing' of the spearhead prior to deposition. Intentional cuts in blade edges are more often found on complete spearheads, not just as a fragment as in this case.

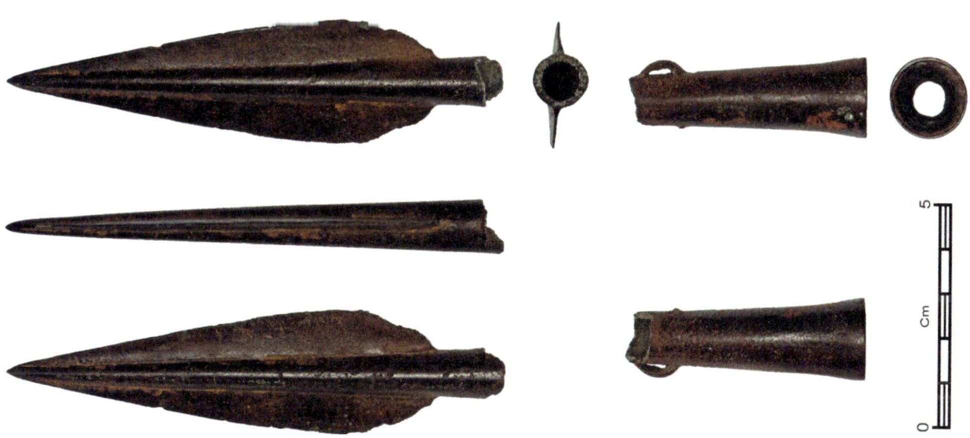

Fig. 130: Late Bronze Age spearhead from Iwerne Minster, Dorset (DOR-DC23F5).

Fig. 131: Late Bronze Age hoard containing a plain leaf-shaped spearhead and a lunate-opening spearhead. Found at Trevethin, Torfaen (NMGW-3EA2A8).

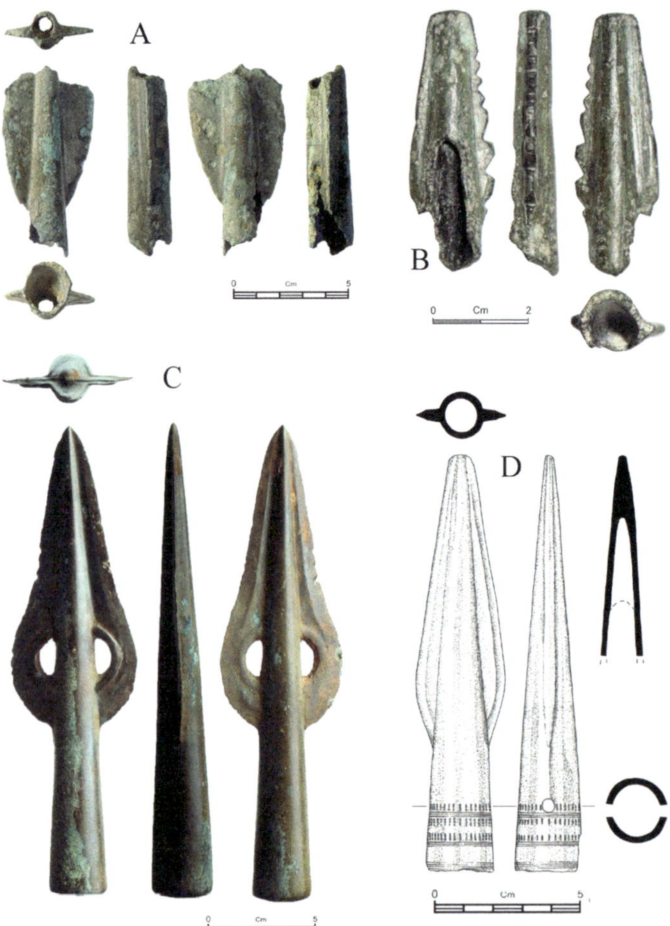

Fig. 132: Spearhead and spearhead fragments from (A) Brearton, North Yorkshire (SWYOR-BB6C1F), (B) Chilcomb, Hampshire (SUR-0FB443), (C) Ufton Nervet, Berkshire (SUR-49AF85), and (D) Wallingford, Oxfordshire (BERK-FCF913).

44. Scabbard chape (BUC-E3E35D)
Late Bronze Age (*c.* 1150–950 BC)
Length: 85.2 mm Width: 40.9 mm Thickness: 14 mm Weight: 48.02 g
Slapton, Buckinghamshire

A 'chape' is the metal cap that is affixed to the bottom tip of a sword or dagger scabbard/sheath by one or more small rivets. While the scabbard itself would have been made from organic material such as leather, the chape was made from metal to give extra protection to the tip of the bladed weapon inside the sheath. Chapes are often decorated and their overall shape and style change over time. A good example for tongue-shaped chapes of the earlier Late Bronze Age comes from Slapton (Buckinghamshire, BUC-E3E35D, Fig. 133) while purse- or bag-shaped chapes like the find from Hinton Martell (Dorset, DOR-BD9AED, Fig. 135D) date to the very end of the Late Bronze Age.

The specimen from Slapton survives intact. It is ogival in shape with a convex top and a lozenge-shaped cross-section. On both sides at half-length there is a circular perforation to the right of its raised central ridge, presumably for the small rivets that affixed the chape to the tip of the scabbard. The inside of the chape is hollow. Tongue-shaped chapes are often made from very thin metal and fragments can be difficult to identify, like the fragments in the hoard found near Ulverston (Cumbria, 2019T558, Fig. 134A) and the larger fragments from Hindon (Wiltshire, WILT-37F8E1, Fig. 135B) and Hatfield Broad Oak (Essex, ESS-6B22A3, Fig. 135C). However, occasionally, larger examples survive (Chedzoy, Somerset, SOMDOR-9ADF54, Fig. 135A). Later Bronze Age chapes are much smaller and

Fig. 133: Scabbard chap from Slapton, Buckinghamshire (BUC-E3E35D).

named after their shape bag-, purse- or boat-shaped chapes, like this complete example from Hinton Martell (Dorset, DOR-BD9AED, Fig. 135D). Both types of chapes may be found single and as part of Late Bronze Age hoards. Another type of 'chape' are ferrules, which are the caps of spears and sit on the terminal that is at the opposite end of the spearhead. They are usually tubular in shape and undecorated, like the example found in the Broadland Hoard (Norfolk, NMS-F1BBE1, Fig. 134B).

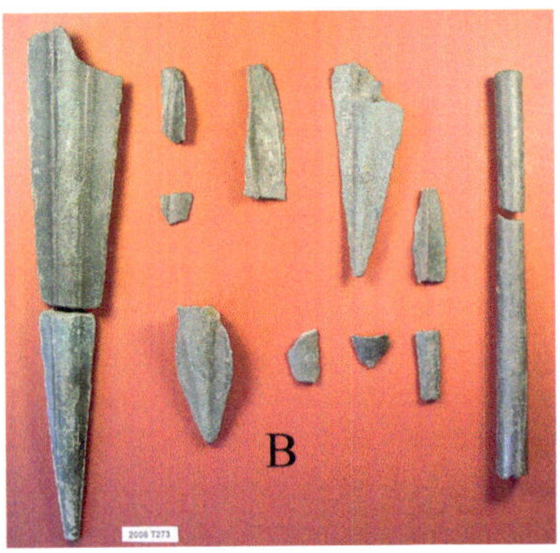

Fig. 134: A: The Ulverston Hoard (Cumbria, 2019T558) includes a large number of broken-up tongue-shaped chapes. B: The Broadland Hoard (Norfolk, NMS-F1BBE1) includes a ferrule (far right) and spearhead fragments.

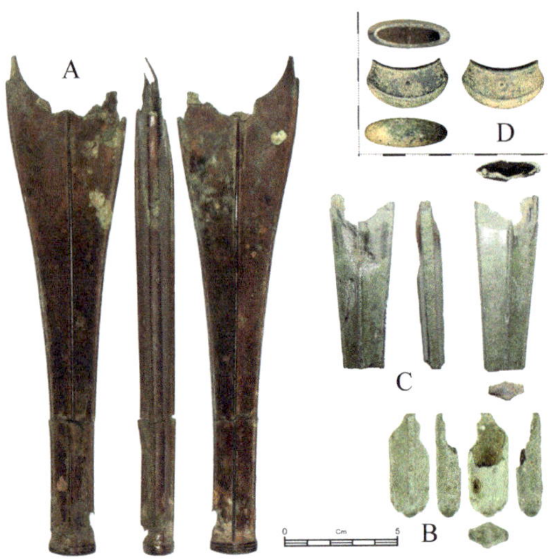

Fig. 135: Incomplete tongue-shaped chapes were recorded from (A) Chedzoy, Somerset (SOMDOR-9ADF54), (B) Hindon, Wiltshire (WILT-37F8E1) and (C) Hatfield Broad Oak, Essex (ESS-6B22A3). The boat- or purse-shaped shape comes from Hinton Martell, Dorset (DOR-BD9AED).

45. Shield (SF-EoD9C8)
Late Bronze Age (*c.* 1300–975 BC)
Thickness: 0.77 mm Diameter: 600 mm
Lakenheath, Suffolk

This incomplete shield was discovered near Lakenheath (Suffolk, SF-EoD9C8, Fig. 136). It dates from the Later Bronze Age and is the only one recorded on the Portable Antiquities Scheme's database. The shield is circular in form, hammered to create a thin disc that in places measures 0.77 mm in thickness. The exterior diameter of the rim is approximately 600 mm. The rim itself rolled forwards onto the front face of the shield. It has a prominent central boss, which is conical in form with vertical sides that are decorated with double concentric grooves. It is missing parts of the central boss and surrounding area, as well as most of the handle. Damage to opposing sides of the rim indicate it has at one stage been partially bent or folded, although it is unclear whether this was deliberate or as a result of deposition. The shield's size and form indicate that it belongs to a group of shields known as Type Yetholm. This type of shield is a typically insular British type of which twenty-six examples are known to date. Shields such as this would have been manufactured by hammering a blank into a thin sheet disc, perhaps using a wooden mould to form the concentric ribs. The circular bosses would have been added through the use of a punch, hence their uniformity in size and shape, and slightly uneven distribution around the bands. The detachable bosses on the central band would have enabled the attachment of a copper-alloy handle to the shield, with the tabs on the back of the detachable bosses probably to allow the shield to be carried on a leather strap. This shield was recovered from waterlogged fen-edge contexts and is currently the only known example from Suffolk.

Fig. 136: Incomplete shield discovered near Lakenheath, Suffolk (SF-EoD9C8).

46. Moustache-shaped object (NMGW-AF1FCC)
Middle Bronze Age to Earliest Iron Age (*c.* 1500–650 BC)
Length: 23.5 mm Height: 22.9 mm Width: 21.5 mm Thickness: 13.1 mm
Weight: 18 g
Llantilio Crossenny, Monmouthshire

This is a group of enigmatic objects that are very distinct. One of them was found at Llantilio Crossenny (Monmouthshire, NMGW-AF1FCC, Fig. 137) and due to their seemingly standardised shape they are generally referred to as 'moustache-shaped objects'. Unfortunately, even though they are so distinct and easily recognisable, they are very poorly understood in terms of function and date. Their form is remarkably consistent, being bi-lobed and rounded, often with a moulded ribbed decoration and two projecting prongs. The two arms may be V-shaped, as in the example from Llantilio Crossenny, or much wider as in the specimens found at Wendover (Buckinghamshire, NARC-6A4546, Fig. 138A) and Clanfield (Oxfordshire, HAMP-6F4C45, Fig. 138B). In some examples they are, however, almost parallel, for example from Kingston Bagpuize (Oxfordshire, BERK-C3E5A3, Fig. 139). Nonetheless, they all share the tapering arms, the moulded grooves and the undecorated band between the two arms, as well as the central perforation. There is an example from a Middle Bronze Age context at Clay Farm, Cambridgeshire, and another was found in the multi-period Salisbury Hoard, suggesting a Middle Bronze to Early Iron Age date for these enigmatic objects. They generally resemble Early Iron Age winged chapes, which is why they are sometimes referred to as 'chapes'. However, not all of them are hollow and not all of them have two arms, which would make their interpretation as chapes unlikely (see No. 44).

Fig. 137: A moustache-shaped ornament from Llantilio Crossenny, Monmouthshire (NMGW-AF1FCC).

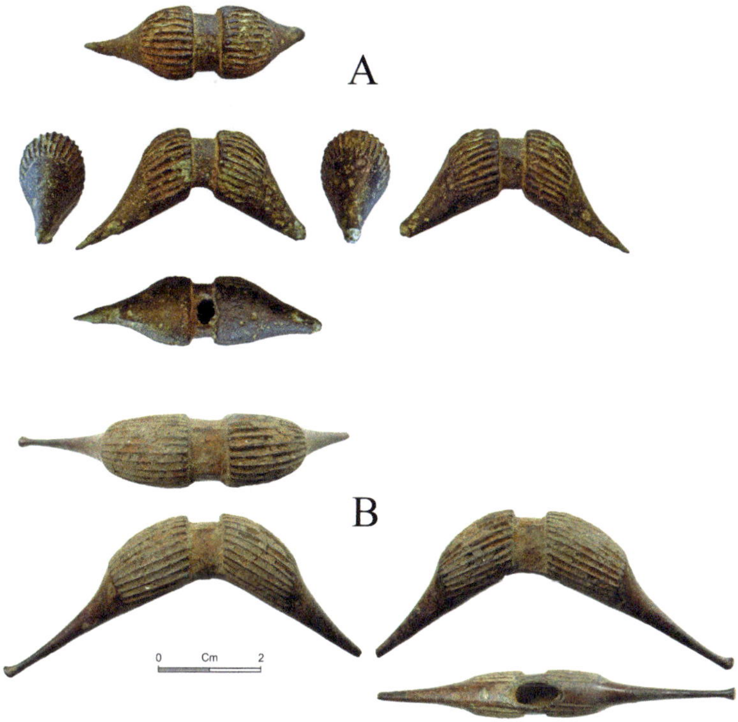

Fig. 138: Two moustache-shaped objects from (A) Wendover (Buckinghamshire, NARC-6A4546) and (B) Clanfield (Oxfordshire, HAMP-6F4C45).

Fig. 139: A moustache-shaped object from Kingston Bagpuize, Oxfordshire (BERK-C3E5A3).

47. Bracelets (NCL-9F9F92/2005T120)

Late Bronze Age (C14 dated to between 1000–840 BC)
The Collette Hoard, Northumberland

Late Bronze Age bracelets can be difficult to identify if not found in association with other Late Bronze Age objects. They are not normally as elaborately decorated as Middle Bronze Age bracelets and armlets, which are often decorated with incised or moulded ornaments or may be twisted (see Nos 24–26). Late Bronze Age bracelets appear to be predominantly penannular (that means that they have an opening on one side) and often have expanding, slightly trumpet-shaped terminals as can be seen on the gold bracelet from Soberton (Hampshire, HAMP-5E48D1, Fig. 141A) or, somewhat less pronounced, on the bronze bracelet fragments in the Collette Hoard (Northumberland, NCL-9F9F92, Fig. 140). As a Late Bronze Age assemblage the Collette Hoard contained socketed axes, a bifid razor, a gouge, a spearhead fragment, a terret, potential ceramic crucible fragments and the fragments of at least six plain bracelets or armlets, at least two of which had expanding terminals. The hoard was C14 dated to between 1000–840 BC. A smaller hoard containing three gold bracelets was discovered at Milton Keynes (PAS-833958, Fig. 142). Here, five gold jewellery items – two gold neck rings and three gold bracelets – were found in an undecorated pottery vessel. The two neck rings were unusual in that they were decorated with incised decoration suggesting an Atlantic/Irish or even Iberian connection. Another unique ornament resembling a bracelet with a potentially Irish background was found at Dymock (Gloucestershire, NMGW-7ECFB8, Fig. 141B). This object, which was identified as a 'dress fastener', is a ring with very large, flat-circular terminals. It appears unfinished with remnants of the casting jets still intact. These so-called 'dress fasteners' are found in Late Bronze Age contexts but are of uncertain function. They are generally made of gold

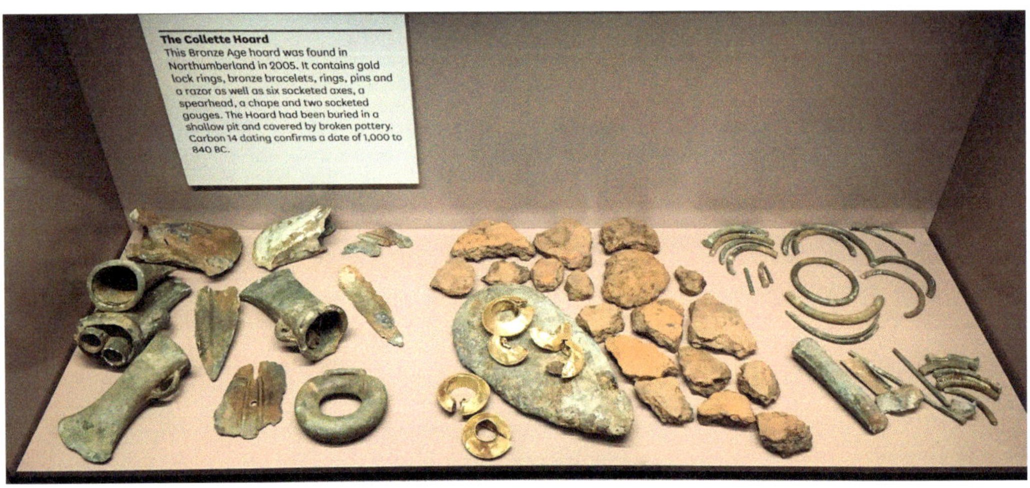

Fig. 140: The Collette Hoard, Northumberland (NCL-9F9F92), was radiocarbon-dated to 1000–840 BC. It contained bronze tools, ingots, gold 'lock rings' and a number of bracelet fragments. (Photo: Abigail Baker)

and found in Ireland and Scotland, with outliers from Yorkshire and Norfolk. Bronze examples are much rarer than gold ones, for example in the Mountrivers Hoard (County Cork, Ireland) and the Poolewe Hoard (Ross and Cromarty, Scotland).

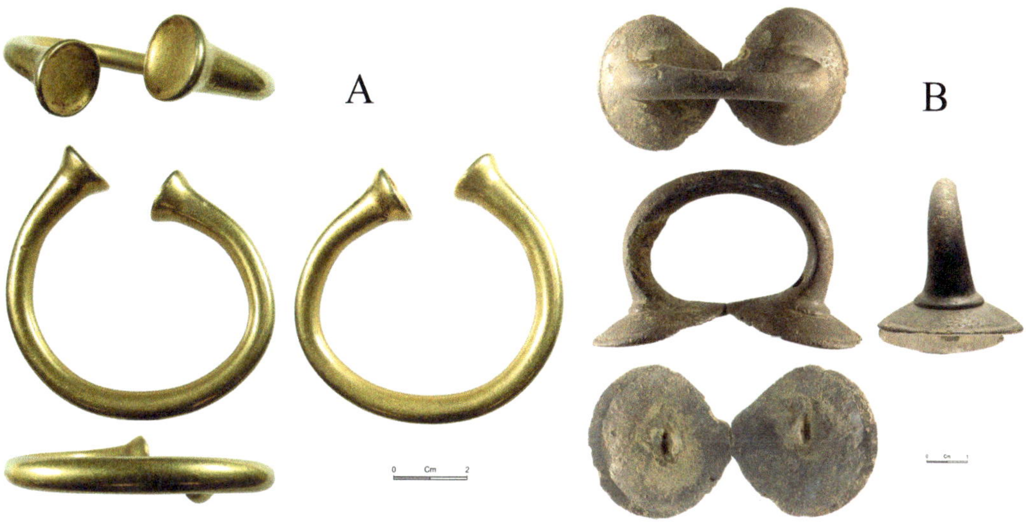

Fig. 141: Two different types of Late Bronze Age bracelet: A: Gold bracelet from Soberton (Hampshire, HAMP-5E48D1). B: 'Dress fastener' from Dymock, Gloucestershire (NMGW-7ECFB8).

Fig. 142: Small hoard containing three gold penannular bracelets from Milton Keynes (PAS-833958).

48. Lock rings (LVPL-5DFE32/LVPL-229426)
Late Bronze Age (*c.* 1000–800 BC)
1. Length: 38.02 mm Width: 29.97 mm Thickness: 11.71 mm Weight: 8.9 g
2. Length: 35.6 mm Width: 41.5 mm Thickness: 11.6 mm Weight: 8.4 g
Rossett, Wrexham

Late Bronze Age 'lock rings' are small penannular gold ornaments presumably worn in or around one's hair – hence the name. They are a distinct class of personal ornament made from gold plates, secured together by binding strips to create a hollow penannular ring with triangular cross-section. The three gold plates, technically termed 'face plates', are sometimes decorated with repoussé decoration or with fine concentric incised lines imitating fine wire work (e.g. Hambledon, Hampshire, SUSS-5EA230, Fig. 143B, and Whissendine, Rutland, ESS-5ECCA2, Fig. 143A). Recently, a radiocarbon date has been obtained from a sample directly associated with a large hoard of bronze artefacts and six gold lock rings from near Berwick upon Tweed, Northumberland (see No. 46.). The sample of wood, surviving within the haft of a socketed axe, provided a date of *c.* 1000–840 BC. Lock rings are very intricately decorated and the quality of workmanship is generally very high. As mentioned above, their precise function as personal ornaments

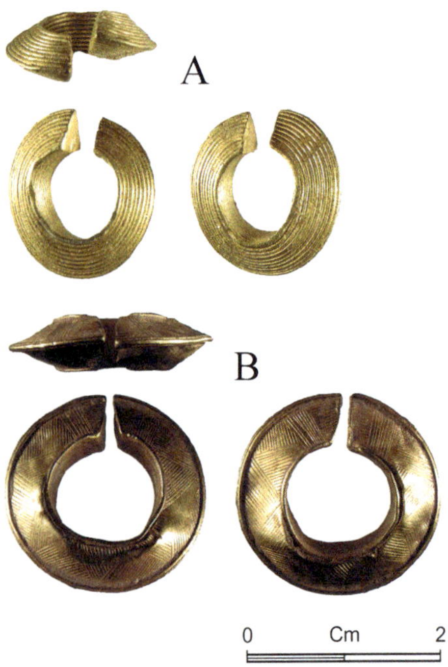

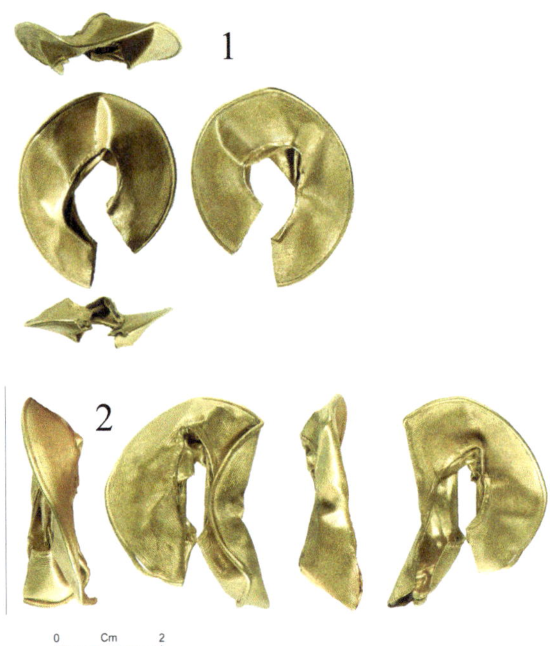

Above left: Fig. 143: Two gold 'lock rings' with incised and repousse decoration from (A) Whissendine, Rutland (ESS-5ECCA2) and (B) Hambledon, Hampshire (SUSS-5EA230).

Above right: Fig. 144: 'Lock rings are found in pairs, like these from Rossett, Wrexham (1: LVPL-5DFE32, 2: LVPL-229426).

remains uncertain; they may have been hair ornaments or possibly earrings, which would be supported by them often being found in pairs, like the two examples from Rossett (Wrexham, LVPL-5DFE32/LVPL-229426, Fig. 144). What is generally agreed is that they denoted wealth and high status within Late Bronze Age society. They are found singly and, quite often, in small hoards with other gold and bronze metalwork, for example with a gold armlet and fragment of a socketed axe (Urswick, Cumbria, LANCUM-C98FBF, Fig. 145A) or even hidden inside the socket of a socketed axe (North Cove Suffolk, SF-BDA986, Fig. 145B).

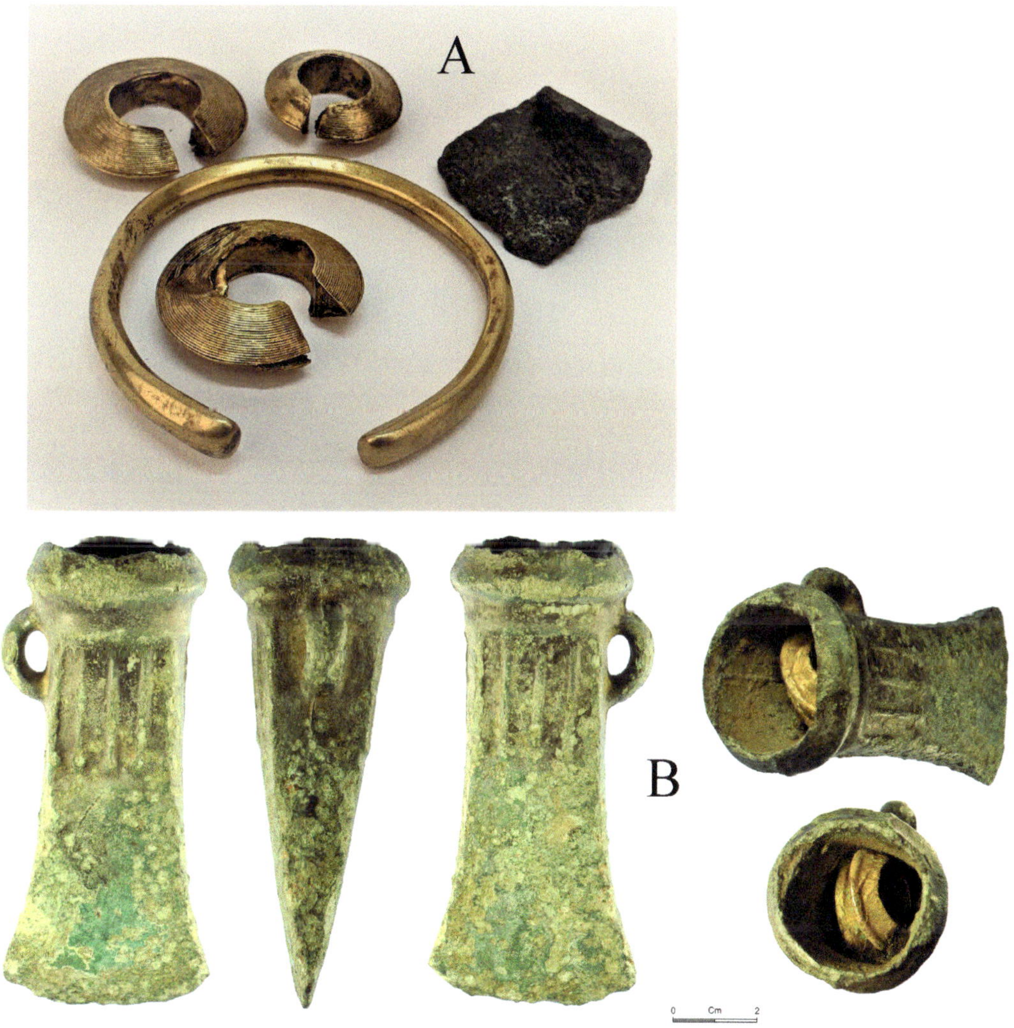

Fig. 145: Two small hoard containing gold lock rings from (A) Urswick, Cumbria (LANCUM-C98FBF) and (B) North Cove, Suffolk (SF-BDA986) where the rings had been hidden inside the socket of a socketed axe.

49. Penannular ring (DUR-B76D9B)
Late Bronze Age (*c.* 1150–800 BC)
Diameter: 18.5 mm Thickness: 7.15 mm Weight: 11.4 g
High Coniscliffe, County Durham

Gold or gold-on-base-metal penannular rings belong to a well-dated Late Bronze Age group of ornaments. Similar to lock rings, their function remains uncertain, although it is likely that they were personal adornments, possibly worn on the ears or nose rather than as hair ornaments like the slightly larger penannular lock rings (see No. 48). The penannular ring from High Coniscliffe (County Durham, DUR-B76D9B, Fig. 146) survives complete with only some corrosion between the terminals. The corrosion indicates that instead of having been made from a solid gold rod, it was made by covering a circular bronze bar with gold sheet and hammering it flat, giving it the appearance of being made from solid gold. The ring was then decorated with silver or silver rich gold wire, which covers the ring in a continuous spiral that provides a stripy effect. Another plated penannular ring was recorded from Martham (Norfolk, NMS-3E8DD8, Fig. 147C); here, the outer plating was damaged and is starting to peel away, revealing the ring's bronze core. A core that lost all its gold plating was recorded from Houghton (Hampshire, HAMP-03E054, Fig. 147A). Unlike the other penannular rings discussed here, this would not constitute treasure if found on its own, as just the base metal remains – all the gold is gone. In contrast, solid gold penannular rings were found at Downton (Wiltshire, SOM-E86C93, Fig. 147B) and, as part of a small hoard, at Cwm Cadnant (Anglesey, NMGW-04216C, Fig. 148). Not all penannular rings are stripy: some are just made from a short length of gold rod, like the example from near Compton (West Sussex, SUSS-585B49, Fig. 147D).

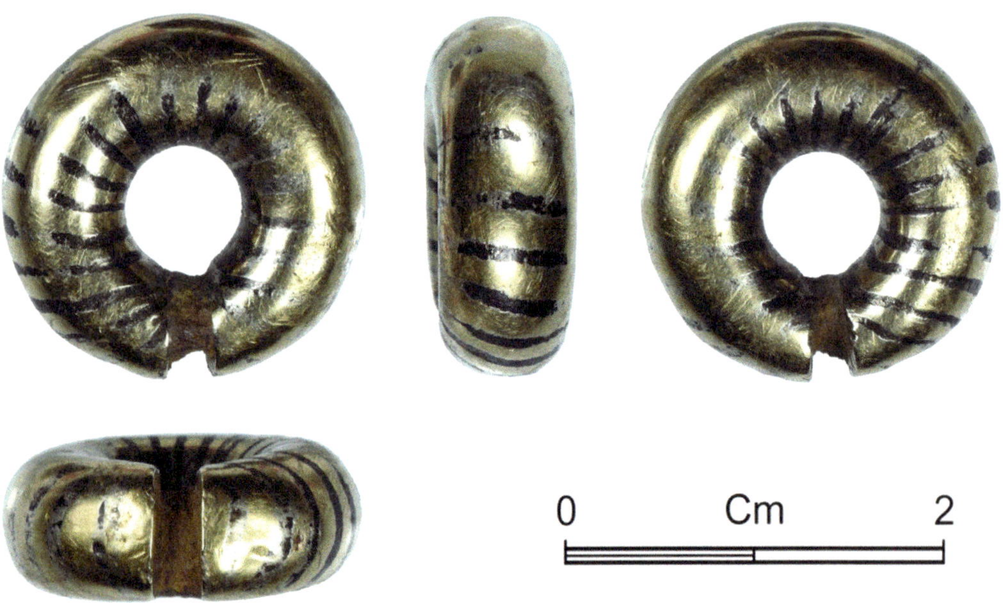

Fig. 146: A penannular ring from High Coniscliffe, County Durham (DUR-B76D9B).

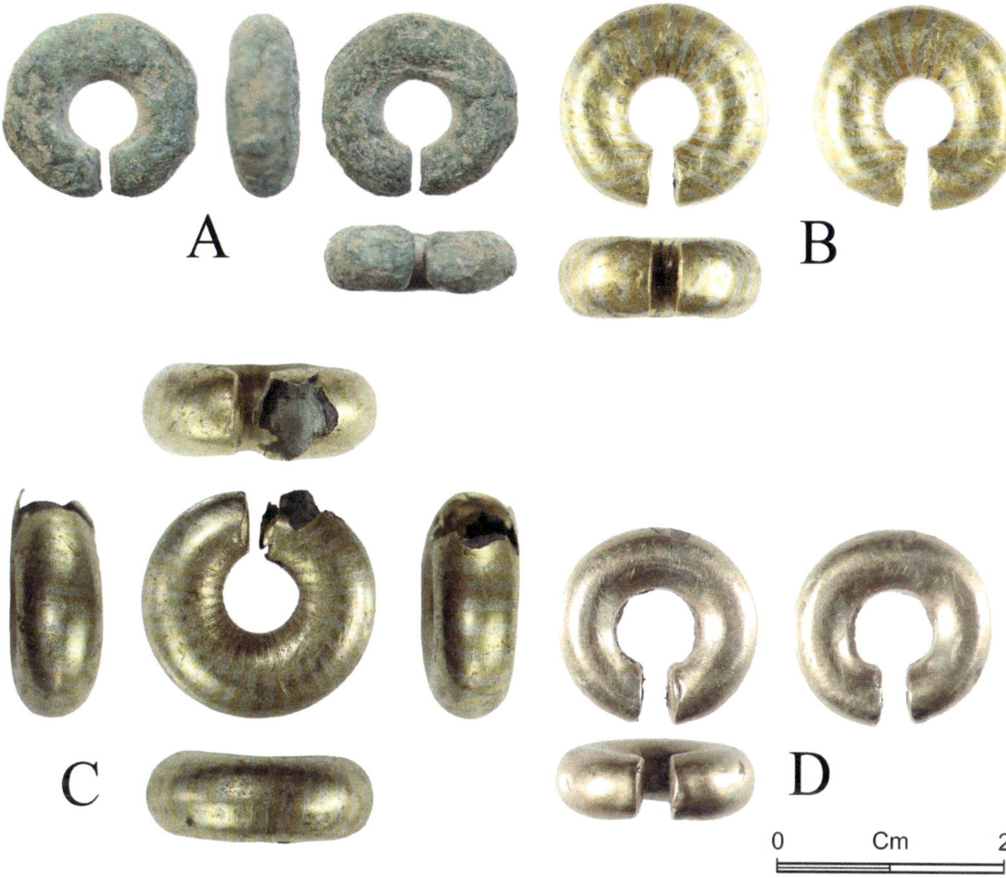

Above: Fig. 147: Four penannular rings from (A) Houghton, Hampshire (HAMP-03E054: bronze core), (B) Downton, Wiltshire (SOM-E86C93, solid gold, stripy), (C) Martham, Norfolk (NMS-3E8DD8, plated penannular ring, stripy) and (D) Compton, West Sussex (SUSS-585B49, made from gold rod).

Right: Fig. 148: A small hoard including a stripy penannular ring from Cwm Cadnant, Anglesey (NMGW-04216C).

50. Cauldron handle (SUR-30F173)
Late Bronze Age (*c.* 1150–800 BC)
Length: 23.57 mm Width: 22.9 mm Thickness: 13.36 mm Weight: 24.19 g
Gravesham, Kent

During the Later Bronze Age and Early Iron Age we are beginning to see evidence for large scale feasting and possible community gatherings. Buckets and large cauldrons made from bronze sheet metal have been found in the past but nothing as large as that has ever been recorded with on the Portable Antiquities Scheme database. However, metal detectorists have uncovered smaller fragments of cauldrons, such as this ribbed cauldron staple fragment from Gravesham (Kent, SUR-30F173, Fig. 149). It probably came from the rim of a bucket or a cauldron; a more complete example, with the ring handle still attached, was found near Saxlingham (Norfolk, SF-832744, Fig. 150A). This larger fragment still preserves small areas of sheet vessel comprising folded sheet of copper alloy that is visible as essentially two sheets on the back face of the attachment plate where it is held in place with a large central flattened circular rivet. The folded sheet extends between the lug and attachment plate, which hold it in place and into the interior aperture of the lug. Here it is visible flat against the lower front surface of the lug's aperture, where it wraps around and holds in place a separately cast copper-alloy rod that is visible at both sides of the handle but now incomplete due to old breaks. Presumably this separate rod extended around the rim helping to strengthen it and give it form. A number of cauldron, staple and ring fragments were found at Salle (Norfolk, NMS-6E1D71, Fig. 150C; photo of staple: Fig. 150B). The staples and ring handles are very similar to those on a well preserved cauldron found with a flesh hook at Feltwell, Norfolk (NHER5191, Norfolk Museum and Archaeology Service accession No. 1961.373). Wood from the socket of the flesh hook was radiocarbon dated to 1390–1120 BC and deposits around the rim were found to be the remains of carbonised food including animal fats. Flesh hooks are equally rare finds on the database, but one was recorded from Saham Toney (Norfolk, NMS-6E1D71, Fig. 151).

Fig. 149: A ribbed cauldron staple fragment from Gravesham, Kent (SUR-30F173).

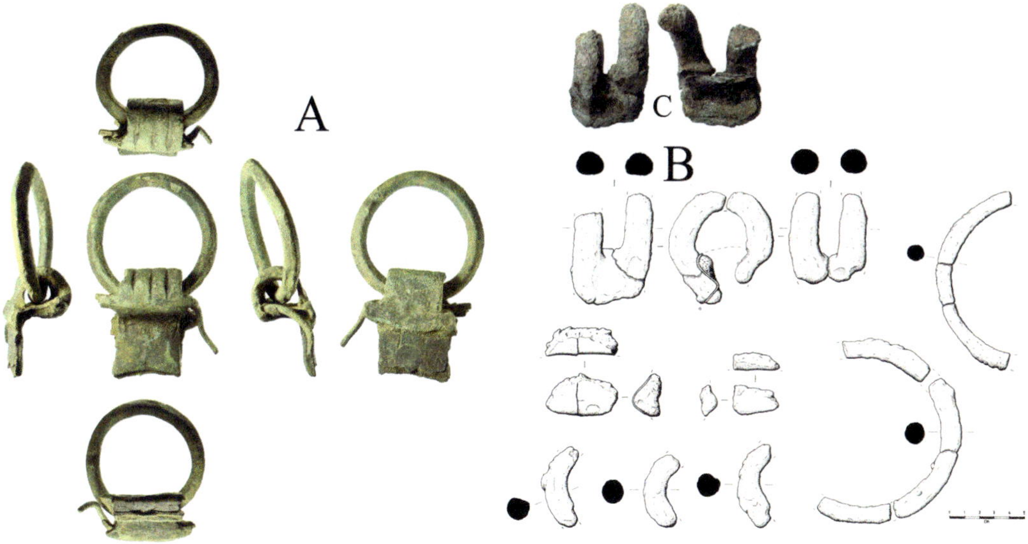

Fig. 150: Cauldron ring handle and staple fragments from (A) Saxlingham, Norfolk (SF-832744) and (C) Salle, Norfolk (NMS-6E1D71). B: Photo of staple fragment from Salle.

Fig. 151: Flesh hook fragment from Saham Toney, Norfolk (NMS-6E1D71).

Bibliography

Bowman, S., and Needham, S., 'The Dunaverney and Little Thetford Flesh-hooks: History, Technology and their Position within the Later Bronze Age Atlantic Zone Feasting Complex', *The Antiquaries Journal*, Vol. 87 (2007), 53–108

Burgess, C., and Gerloff, S., 'The Dirks and Rapiers of Great Britain and Ireland', *Prähistorische Bronzefunde*, Abteilung IV 7 (München: C. H. Beck'sche Verlagsbuchandlung, 1981)

Burgess, C., and Colquhoun, I., *The Swords of Britain* (München: C. H. Beck'sche Verlagsbuchandlung, 1988)

Davis, R., *Basal-looped Spearheads, Typology, Chronology, Context and Use*, British Archaeological Reports International Series 1497 (Oxford: BAR Publishing, 2006)

Davis, R., *The Early and Middle Bronze Age Spearheads of Britain*, Prähistorische Bronzefunde, Abteilung V.5 (Stuttgart: Franz Steiner Verlag, 2012)

Davis, R., *The Late Bronze Age Spearheads of Britain*, Prähistorische Bronzefunde, Abteilung V.7 (Stuttgart: Franz Steiner Verlag, 2015)

Eogan, G., 'The Associated Finds of Gold Bar Torcs', *Journal of the Royal Society of Antiquaries of Ireland*, 98 (2) (1967), 129–175

Eogan, G., ''Lock-rings' of the Late Bronze Age', *Proceedings of the Royal Irish Academy*, 67C (1969), 93–148

Eogan, G., *The Hoards of the Irish Later Bronze Age* (Dublin: University College Dublin, 1983)

Eogan, G., *The Accomplished Art: Gold and Gold-working in Britain and Ireland during the Bronze Age (c. 2300–650 BC)* (Oxford: Oxbow Monograph 42, 1995)

Fox, C., 'The Socketed Bronze Sickles of the British Isles; with special reference to an unpublished specimen from Norwich', *Proceedings of the Prehistoric Society*, 5 (1939), 222–248

Fox, C., 'The Non-socketed Bronze Sickles of Britain', *Archaeologia Cambrensis*, Vol. 96 (1941), 136–162

Gerloff, S., *The Early Bronze Age Daggers in Great Britain: and a Reconsideration of the Wessex Culture*, Prähistorische Bronzefunde, Abteilung VI.2 (München: C. H. Beck'sche Verlagsbuchandlung, 1975)

Gerloff, S., *Atlantic Cauldrons and Buckets of the Late Bronze and Early Iron Ages in Western Europe. With a Review of Comparable Vessels from Central Europe and Italy*, Prähistorische Bronzefunde, Abteilung II.18 (Stuttgart: Franz Steiner Verlag, 2010)

Hartmann, A., *Prähistorische Goldfunde aus Europa II: Studien zu den Anfängen der Metallurgie 5* (Berlin, 1982)

Hermann, R., Crellin, R., Uckelmann, M., Wang, Q. and Dolfini, A. (eds.), *Bronze Age Combat. An Experimental Approach*, British Archaeological Reports International Series 2967 (Oxford: BAR Publishing, 2020)

Horn, C., and Kristiansen, K. (eds.), *Warfare in Bronze Age Society* (Cambridge: Cambridge University Press, 2018)

Jockenhövel, A., *Die Rasiermesser in Westeuropa*, Prähistorische Bronzefunde, Abteilung VIII.3 (München: C.H. Beck'sche Verlagsbuchhandlung, 1980)

La Niece, S., and Cartwright, C., 'Bronze Age Gold Lock-rings with Cores of Wax and Wood' in Kienlin, T. L., and Roberts, B. W. (eds.), *Metals and Societies: Studies in Honour of Barbara S. Ottaway* (Bonn: Universitätsforschungen zur prähistorischen Archäologie, 2009), 307–312

Meeks, N. D., Craddock, P. T., and Needham, S. P., 'Bronze Age Penannular Gold Rings from the British Isles: Technology and Composition, *Jewellery Studies* 11 (2008), 1–30

O'Brien, W., and O'Driscoll, J., *Hillforts, Warfare and Society in Bronze Age Ireland* (Oxford: Archaeopress Publishing Ltd, 2017)

O'Connor, B., *Cross Channel Relations in the Later Bronze Age*, British Archaeological Reports (British Series) 91 (Oxford: BAR Publishing, 1980)

O'Connor, B., 'The earliest Scottish metalwork since Coles. Scotland in ancient Europe: the Neolithic and Early Bronze Age of Scotland in their European Context' (Edinburgh: Society of Antiquaries of Scotland, 2004), 205–216.

O'Connor, B., 'Llyn Fawr metalwork in Britain: A Review' in C. Haselgrove and R. Pope, (eds.), *The Earlier Iron Age in Britain and the near Continent* (Oxford, 2007), 64-79

Ottaway, B., and Roberts, B., 'The Emergence of Metalworking' in A. Jones (ed.) *Prehistoric Europe. Theory and Practice* (Chichester: Wiley-Blackwell, 2008), 193–225

Pearce, S., *Bronze Age Metalwork in Southern Britain* (Aylesbury: Shire Publications, 1984)

Schmidt, P., and Burgess, C., *The Axes of Scotland and Northern England*, Prähistorische Bronzefunde, Abteilung IX.7 (München: C. H. Beck'sche, Verlagsbuchandlung, 1981)

Taylor, J. J., 'Lunulae Reconsidered', *Proceedings of the Prehistoric Society*, 36 (1970), 38–81.

Taylor, J. J., *Bronze Age Goldwork of the British Isles* (Cambridge: Cambridge University Press, 1980)

Timberlake, S., 'Copper mining and metal production at the beginning of the British Bronze Age' in P. Clark (ed.), *Bronze Age Connections: Cultural Contact in Prehistoric Europe* (Oxford: Oxbow Books, 2009), 94–121

Uckelmann, M., and Mödlinger, M., *Bronze Age Warfare: Manufacture and Use of Weaponry*, British Archaeological Reports 2255 (Oxford: BAR Publishing, 2011)

Useful Websites

Portable Antiquities Scheme Website: https://finds.org.uk/database

Must Farm: http://www.mustfarm.com/Bronze Age settlement excavation

AHRC Research Network on gold in Britain's auriferous regions, 2450–800 BC: https://www.nms.ac.uk/collections-research/our-research/featured-projects/prehistoric-gold/

Experimental Archaeology and Bronze Age Experience: https://www.ancientcraft.co.uk/Archaeology/bronze-age/bronzeage.html

The Prehistoric Society Teaching Website: https://theprehistoricsociety.school.blog/welcome-to-the-prehistoric-society-teaching-and-learning-resource-blog/teaching-resources/

Stone Tools, e.g.: https://www.orkneystonetools.org.uk/

Great Orme Mines: https://www.greatormemines.info/